A BIRD COLLECTOR'S MEDLEY

BY

E. C. ARNOLD, M.A.

With Twelve Coloured and Eight Collotype Plates from Drawings by the Author, and barious Illustrations in the Text

LONDON

WEST, NEWMAN & CO., 54, HATTON GARDEN

SIMPKIN, MARSHALL, HAMILTON, KENT & CO.

—

1907

PREFACE.

THIS book is dedicated to my brothers and to those who have been shore-shooting with me in Norfolk and elsewhere, and whose names in some cases appear in the text.

It is intended mainly for the edification of amateur collectors and shore-shooters, though it is possible that some, who have visited the author's bird collection in the Eastbourne Institute, may feel inclined to extend their acquaintance with the occupants of its cases by a perusal of these pages, in which mention is made of their capture. Some of the pictures also are intended to recall scenes in the collection.

Despite all that has been said against it, I venture to think that in this luxurious age no form of sport is more deserving of encouragement than that which leads its votaries to face the hardships and discomforts which will almost certainly be encountered by those who seek their quarry along the shore.

EASTBOURNE COLLEGE:
October, 1907.

CONTENTS.

LIST OF FULL-PAGE ILLUSTRATIONS.

CHAPTER I.

INTRODUCTORY.

"Anceps quidquid agit nostri est farrago libelli."

To TAKE up the cudgels on behalf of the amateur bird collector may seem in these days a somewhat Quixotic enterprise. Time was when the possession of a good collection of stuffed birds tended to distinguish a man as a Naturalist; to-day he is more likely to find himself regarded as a cold-blooded and heartless butcher. Books, periodicals, papers, and last, but not least, those very ladies who adorn their bonnets with the stuffed effigies of Terns or Bullfinches slaughtered in the breeding season—all these combine to abuse him; and certainly, if words could effect it, the collector would soon become as rare as, or rarer than, the Great Auk itself. Still the advertisement of " Collector's guns," " Collector's handbooks," &c., with which one is daily confronted, would seem to show that the genus as yet survives, and long may it continue to do so!

I have no desire to hold a brief for the type of man who buys his specimens from a dealer, and confines his personal efforts to labelling and arranging them in a cabinet. It goes without saying that this style of collecting does infinite harm, inasmuch as it encourages the wholesale slaughter of rare birds, to keep up the stock-in-trade of the so-called London " Naturalist."

But the man who shoots, stuffs, and cases his birds himself stands, I think, upon a very different footing. If he happens to be a butcher, it is certainly not because of his collecting proclivities; in fact, he is usually contented with one pair of any given species, if only because he has no room wherein to stow away a larger number, and when he has once secured a couple, the remaining members of the tribe may run the gauntlet of his ambush with impunity. " Why can't he be content to use only his field-glasses ? " says some eminent naturalist, who has possibly amassed a fine private collection in his youth, and has now taken up the fashionable cry. For the very good reason that the ordinary man, who is fond of birds, cannot spend the year in travelling from place to place to look at them in their native haunts. He therefore perhaps

B

finds time for one, or the at most two, short shooting expeditions, which he plans out with other kindred spirits.   The birds are sought for, shot, and stuffed, and afterwards treasured as mementos of a healthful and enjoyable holiday, mementos on which the eye can be feasted during the remainder of the working year.

I have never yet come across the collector who was not delighted to show his birds to anyone interested in the subject, and much pleasure is thus afforded to others, who may have had no opportunity of visiting the localities where they are found.   Lastly, he can end by presenting them to some museum. We all sneered once at museums and stuffed birds in general ; we contrasted the live bird with the resurrected "specimen," and we still point the finger of scorn at the old-fashioned taxidermist, who, confining his ambition to "setting up" a skin, does indeed produce some weird, uncanny representations of nature.   But things are changing fast nowadays, and it is ridiculous to maintain that an examination of the cases at South Kensington, or the Booth Museum at Brighton, can give aught but pleasure and instruction to the visitor.

Should a local museum be wanting, one of those which are now being started in our leading schools may perhaps appeal to the "collector" as a suitable haven for his trophies ; but, be this as it may, I propose to give some account of the way in which an ordinary collection is got together, and of the pleasures and disappointments which await the collector himself.   The mania often seizes a boy while still at school.   He rigs up a "catty," and patrols the fields in search of a victim to commence upon.   A fortunate shot lays low a Starling, and solemn preparations are made for stuffing it.   Five minutes after the start the bird is a hopeless wreck, but your Briton knows not when he's beat, and perseveres with grim obstinacy to the bitter end.   There emerges at length that well-known abortion—a stuffed skin, with air-holes to ventilate the tow, wings pendant, and a few feathers distributed in uneven bunches before and behind.   It is decided that "it is not worth while putting in the eyes," and some weeks afterwards the specimen is definitely discarded.

All things, however, must have a beginning, and, as bird-stuffing is more a matter of care and perseverance than innate skill, the would-be Waterton has probably obtained a fair amount of proficiency by the time that he proceeds to the 'Varsity, or any similar abode.   Here he substitutes a walking-stick gun for a catapult, and finds that the smaller canes are most serviceable weapons for dealing with birds of the Finch type, as they do so little damage to the skin.

In certain emergencies the collector will condescend to spread the wily noose, but here he has serious difficulties to contend with.   It is easy enough to set snares for a Jay or a Magpie, but it is quite another matter, if a keeper comes across them, to persuade him that they are not intended for a Partridge. In fact, the collector will find that inland he is duly appreciated nowhere. " Disturbing the birds " is the lightest charge that will be brought against him, and he had better migrate early to his natural resort, the sea shore.

Here, especially in winter, he will be received with open arms as the legitimate victim of some local gunner and his family ; and if he comes of a stock that is proof against damp beds, and possesses the digestion of an ostrich, he may pass a very enjoyable time in the pursuit of Ducks, Divers, Grebes, &c., as well as the ordinary shore birds. On the whole, however, the months of August and September are the best from the collecting point of view. The autumn migration is then at its height, and, in addition to the Waders, many inland species may at that time be met with on the coast.

A few hints may be useful. A fishing village is apt to be short of provisions. I have known places where they only kill an animal when a customer has been found to bespeak every joint of the carcass, and therefore I have found it advisable to take with me a few tinned tongues and some good tea. Remember, too, that "Quaker Oats" emerge from the culinary operations of the rustic wife with fewer lumps than does ordinary porridge; and don't believe the assertions of your hostess that she can serve up Redshanks, &c., so that they cannot be told from Snipe. I never yet met one that could do it.

CHAPTER II.

SHORE SHOOTING ON FOOT.

SHORE SHOOTING may take several forms; you may, especially in the autumn, tramp the muds and marshes on foot; you may explore the estuary and its creeks in a flat-bottomed boat or gunning punt; or you may charter a sailing boat, cross the bar, and venture forth on the open sea. In the first two cases the sport will be chiefly amongst the Waders; in the latter there is in winter time a reasonable prospect of meeting with some Duck and Divers, while in summer, if there are cliffs in the neighbourhood, some variety may be picked up in the way of a rock bird.

If it is decided to go on foot, there should be no half-measures. The man who sallies forth equipped with spats and gaiters, and means jumping the drains, may indeed ward off a liver attack, and will certainly make away with much shoe leather, but as for shots, not a bird worth killing will wait till he comes within range. No: the only sensible way of doing things is to discard all clothing below a pair of old shorts, put on sand-shoes to protect the feet from small crustacea, and descend into the drains themselves. The mention of a drain may suggest to some a sort of "cloaca maxima," or other such horror; but the term is used to denote those channels which the sea eats out amidst the saltings, and which have nothing objectionable about them beyond the inherent stickiness of the mud. One soon gets to know the likely corners, and grand shots may be obtained as you come round them, more particularly if there happen to be any Greenshanks in the neighbourhood.

For real temper-testing qualities commend me to the Greenshank. It is a sufficiently rare bird to make the ordinary collector consider it a prize, while it is possessed of an extraordinary wariness which lends a peculiar charm to its pursuit. How well I remember my first long and unsuccessful chase! For four consecutive days we saw two Greenshanks in the marshes. Once they rose just as we were jumping a dyke; once a Redshank put them up when we had nearly crawled within range; a third good chance was fumbled away through sheer anxiety; and then, to crown all, the village blacksmith got up early the next morning, shot both, and ate them! It may be worth

E. C. ARNOLD PINXT.] LIFE IN A TIDAL DRAIN. (*Greenshank and Curlew Sandpipers.*)

[WEST NEWMAN.

remarking here that Greenshanks on the wing can be told from Redshanks by their longer bodies and more mellow note.

Apart from the probability of stalking something in the drain itself, perhaps a Little Stint or a Curlew-Sandpiper, there is also the chance of seeing some good Wader on the wing in the distance, in which case you can crouch under the nearer bank and try to whistle him over. A newly arrived Godwit or Whimbrel will in the majority of cases respond, and, if you only

IN A TIDAL DRAIN.

keep still long enough, a good shot is almost sure to result. In fact, merely waiting in a favourite channel is in most cases attended with more success than promiscuous following, especially late in the day when you have discovered the direction of the evening flight. But it is not such an easy matter as it would appear. The mud is so soft that to remain stationary for more than a few seconds is to be submerged up to the knees with the prospect of being converted into a fixture, if you happen to be far from the bank. "*Facilis descensus Averni*," glibly murmurs Virgil; and the remark is equally true of

the mud at the bottom of a tidal drain.   But the more prosaic question which
confronts the engulfed shooter is, " how to get out again ? "   It is difficult to
prescribe for such an emergency ; but as, supposing the tide to be on the
turn, the position is unpleasant in the extreme, my own experience may
perhaps be of service to the unwary.

The only time I was ever actually stuck—within, by the way, two yards
of the suggestive skeleton of a sheep—a friend succeeded in bringing an oar
and throwing it to me.   I raised myself on it with my arms, and was surprised
at the ease with which my feet came out.   The mud seemed to have no real
holding power, one was detained only by the impossibility of getting any shove
off from the bottom.   It occurred to me afterwards that I might have used my
gun as I did the oar, and, though I have never yet sacrificed it to prove the
truth of this theory, I have little doubt but that it would work.

As a last resort, it is popularly maintained that the captive should recline
on his back, pull up his legs, if he can, and then shuffle off after the manner
of a serpent ; but as prevention in the case of so dire a remedy is certainly
better than cure, it is wisest to be provided with the skin of an old football,
which will form a tolerable seat on any projecting piece of solid mud, and if
the shooter throws down a plentiful supply of samphire on the slime beneath
his feet, he will be able to jump up when the birds are within range and get a
safe and comfortable standing shot.   Of course, many people may consider this
mud-larking programme altogether beneath them, but I can at all events vouch
for its efficacy, while, as for the dirt, one walk into the open sea at the finish,
and not a sign of it remains to be seen.   The only serious objection that I have
ever experienced is the chance of being stung by one of the numerous bees
which abound amidst the samphire at this season ; and on this account it is
advisable to take with you a small lump of common soda to rub on the spot
as soon as the sting has been extracted.

The luncheon interval is one that should be made the most of by judiciously
selecting a resting-place either near some frequented creek, or amidst some sand-
hills bordering on the marsh.   The entrance to a rabbit burrow will form a
most comfortable arm-chair for the weary, and, as you lie ensconced within
its grateful cavity, it is astonishing how many birds, the majority of them from
behind, will fly within range of a ready gun.   Curiosity seems often to get
the better of wariness, however constitutional, and I have bagged even the
wily Curlew in this way.

The prospects of sport will be still further enhanced if we have some
dummies to put down at the water's edge.   The chief objection to dummies
is the difficulty of conveying the ordinary sort about.   I once invented some

which at all events had the merit of being portable. They were made of two pieces of linen cut in the shape of a bird, sewed together so as to leave a hollow interior, and painted as required. Several could be carried in the pocket, and it was easy to stuff them with grass and set them up with wires when the selected spot was reached. These dummies, though not really very life-like, may claim to have deceived the intelligence of one human being at least, the consequences being all but disastrous to their owner. Hidden amongst some

HOME ALONG THE SHORE.

bushes, I had been enjoying a continuous series of most satisfactory shots, when, after a somewhat longer interval, a Whimbrel came sailing up the estuary. Unlike its predecessors, it failed to descend when it saw the dummies, but, checking its flight, hovered high up above them. Despairing of any nearer approach, I at last sprang up and fired. The report had scarcely died away, when a voice behind me remarked with all the delightful *sang froid* of a shore shooter, " Lucky you got up when you did, sir, or I might have taken you on the way." A hurried survey of the situation convinced me that there was reason in his words, and it transpired that the speaker had espied my dummies, and, mistaking them for real birds, had been engaged in stalking them under cover of the very bushes which formed the central figure in my ambuscade, so that I probably owe it to the afore-mentioned Whimbrel that I did not present a carnal impediment to a considerable portion of his charge.

After doing the saltings with thoroughness, it is a good plan to return home along the edge of the sea, for, though shingle will never provide so many shots as mud, the very first-rate shore birds are most often found on it, or by the side of brackish pools not actually in the marsh.   It was in Norfolk, on a strip of most uninviting shingle, frequented only by the Common Tern, that I once came across that rare American visitant the Buff-breasted Sandpiper.

On September 8th, 1899, I was crossing this shingle on my way from the estuary to the bar, when a strange Wader, which had presumably been testing the efficacy of protective coloration, got up almost beneath my feet and slowly flapped along the beach.   Its sandy colour suggested an autumn Dotterel as it rose, so I fired and knocked it over.   As I drew near I thought I had bagged a Reeve, but in the hand it was at once distinguishable by the beautiful marble-like tracery on the under wing.   It was my first really rare Wader, and I shall never forget my sensations.   The wind at the time was north-west, and the weather fine; but we had had a wet south-east wind for the preceding forty-eight hours.   The best account of this species is to be found in Mr. D. G. Elliott's 'North American Shore Birds.'   It is therein stated that the bird prefers fields and grassy plains rather than wet and swampy lands.   He adds that in the breeding season the males are wont to walk about with one wing extended high in the air.   They also spar like fighting cocks, and then tower for about thirty feet with hanging legs.

One such *rencontre* being worth more than fifty ordinary shots, the collector will do well not to despise the apparent barrenness of the shore proper, where he will also have the chance of securing a rarity amongst those passing migrants which skirt without actually stopping on the beach.   Here we may get a glimpse of the Purple Sandpiper hurrying towards some rockier resort, or the Oystercatcher making for his favourite mussel bed, or some Grebe, perchance an Eared or Sclavonian, drifting lazily in with the flowing tide.

The shore shooter who has not obtained leave to go on the marshes inside the sea-wall will find that his best chance of securing a Dotterel is on shingle rather than on mud, and the chance will be a good one if the shingle happens to be dotted with rough rabbit-used turf.   In September, immature

birds are not very uncommon on the Norfolk coast, though doubtless many
people are unable to distinguish them, the plumage being quite unlike that
of the adults. The ground colour is sandy buff, and most of the feathers
on the head and back have black centres, the only features that recall the
spring plumage being the broad eye-stripe, which is now buff instead of
white, and the long tertiaries with their chestnut margins reaching almost to
the end of the wing. Dotterels at this season seldom utter a note, and, when

THE END OF A STALK.

flying, they appear much darker than one would expect. Though tame, and
admitting of a near approach, when once flushed, they fly a long distance
before they alight, though they move slowly, and look as if they were going to
pitch at once. When found on bare shingle they are probably resting, for
they are much more addicted to the short turf inside the sea-wall. At Littlestone I once watched a pair for some time. They were on the golf links, and
seemed to prefer the "lies" where the grass was short. In the distance
they bore a striking resemblance to Mistle Thrushes, which birds, curiously

enough, were present in some numbers on the links. The pose of each species was the same, but the resemblance ceased as soon as the birds moved, the Dotterels progressing with the ordinary smart run of a Plover, quite unlike the ponderous hopping of a Thrush. The only adult Dotterel I have ever secured was shot off shingle in Norfolk, and when I first saw it running ahead of me, it appeared so small that I took it for a large Pipit; moreover it looked dark even for a Dotterel. I have always regarded it as a great piece of luck to have picked up on the shore in September a bird which one associates mainly with the barren hills of the Lake District or the Highlands.

A Temminck's Stint was shot near the same spot; and this strip of shingle, the same which produced the Buff-breasted Sandpiper, is now known to us as the " Historic Strip."

If, as in the case of my pet Norfolk estuary, the district happens to possess a proper sand-bar, an occasional day spent there will not be wasted. Even if the shooter has no boat, he can sit down on a sand-spit or on one of the buoys, which will be left stranded at low water, and, though it may be necessary to wait long for a shot, the chance that comes at last will very likely be a good one. My brother Brandon was always enamoured of the bar, and spent hours there at various times, partly, no doubt, attracted by the lonely grandeur of the scene. His opportunity came at last, and he took it. Flapping slowly along the edge of the breakers, there sailed into view a bird which appeared " half Gull, half Tern." A fortunate shot precipitated it into the water, and while the wind fought the tide and kept it nearly stationary, he undressed and managed to retrieve it before it was carried out. It proved to be a Little Gull, very immature, but for that reason a most beautiful bird. In general colouring it was not unlike an immature Black Tern, but the markings were bolder and much more effective.

The bar is the recognized resort of any Skua that happens to be in the neighbourhood, but of the Skua more anon. It is also the most likely place for a Black Tern or a Sandwich, though the former often wanders beyond the sea-wall, and can be seen hawking over the fresh marshes inside. It is visited at times by Gannets; stray Cormorants cross it, and Shearwaters pass it, but usually out of range. There is always a reasonable chance of meeting with some Sheld-Duck, birds which breed in the adjacent sandhills, and may be seen in spring time escorting their broods down to the shallow water at their base.

In rough weather still more oceanic birds put in an appearance to recoup after their wild struggle with the elements, and amidst the ordinary

F. C. ARNOLD, PHOT.

DOTTERELS.

WEST NEWMAN.

Alcidæ may be found at times a Petrel or a Little Auk. In fact, though a homeward stroll along the shore often means no shots at all, the locality is one in which you may well meet anything; and as the walking, at all events at low tide, is much superior to that across the marsh, it is, all things considered, far the best way of ending up a long day's tramp.

NOTHING ABOUT.

CHAPTER III.

SHORE SHOOTING FROM A BOAT.

THE majority of shooters, at all events those on the wrong side of thirty, will, we imagine, always be attracted by the cleanly comfort of a rowing boat; and there is much to be said for this method of proceeding, always supposing that you can come across that veiitable *rara avis*, a good-tempered, unofficious, non-avaricious boatman.

In the first place, stray birds seem to come nearer to a boat than to a pedestrian; and secondly, one's energies are saved up till the likely spots are reached, instead of being frittered away by carrying one's lunch, and by a tiring tramp over the unproductive ground near the village; thirdly, you can carry with you the materials for making tea; and lastly, the mud-larker may always be stopped short in the midst of some exciting chase by suddenly finding himself at the edge of a creek too deep to be forded.

There are, in fact, few more enjoyable ways of spending a fine day than the one now under discussion, and long shall I remember my own first experience of one such typical and delightful expedition. Starting gaily on the ebb, down a well-known Norfolk estuary, we, though scarcely clear of the houses, were soon engaged in watching the motions of several Common Sandpipers as they pottered about beneath the overhanging banks, their sheeny plumage glistening brightly in the morning sun, when, thump! thump! there was a sudden commotion in the bows, followed by a hasty and ineffectual shot. A Scaup drake had flown into us unawares, and escaped black fate for the nonce at the cost of nothing more serious than a jar to its nervous system. Some minutes later the bow gun spoke again, and a Knot struck the water within a few feet of the boat, while the shooter in the stern wheeled round just in time to drop a Golden Plover which had already left us forty yards in the rear. The sound of the shots brought up a Merlin to see what was happening, but he prudently refrained from any close investigation, and we, of course, began to speculate eagerly as to what we should see when we reached the much lauded mud-flats beyond. But, as often happens, the birds had appeared just where they were not expected, and when we did approach these happy hunting grounds, we had to be content with the boatman's account of what he had shot there on former occasions. Common politeness prevented us from suggesting doubts as to his veracity, but we were dimly conscious that these stories had been told to other customers before, and had at all events lost nothing by the telling.

After lying across the main channel for half an hour without a shot, B—— at length determined on a stroll through some bushes on the chance

STARTING DOWN THE ESTUARY.

of picking up a rare warbler; but fortune seemed to have deserted us for the time, and soon by general consent it was decided to make a further move towards the bar. On the way we shot an immature Common Tern by mistake for a Black one, a mishap which proved a blessing in disguise, for when we reached our destination, and espied two Sandwich Terns in the distance, the fisherman tied our late victim to a string, and, waving it vigorously round his head while he imitated the Sandwich call-note, at length sent it whizzing into the sea. It was an anxious moment as the line fluttered out. At first the birds seemed inclined to disregard the lure, but a second cast proved more successful, and our hopes rose high as the younger of the pair was seen to be heading for the boat. The old bird followed directly, the faint flesh-coloured tinge upon the breast showing clearly as they crossed our bows. We were fortunate in securing both, and they proved to be in splendid plumage—a grand addition to any collection, however choice. It is less easy than one might suppose to distinguish Sandwich Terns by their size, unless they happen to be consorting with another species. Their size depends so much on the height at which they are flying, that their note affords a far surer means of identification. It is a distinctly double note (kee-wit), very distinct from the long-drawn " shree " of the Common Tern or the series of short single notes uttered by the Arctic.

I may mention here that a handkerchief knotted in the centre round a stone is practically as good a decoy as a dead Tern, and will save the life of many an undeserving bird. Lunch was the next item on the programme, and while the victuals disappeared with business-like rapidity, we admired the fine diving powers of several Gannets which were fishing in company outside the bar. They were immature birds in the brown plumage. But all the artifices of our companion were in vain set forth for their allurement—they remained, as did some Skuas, hopelessly out of range throughout the day. The Sandwich Terns proved therefore the *pièce de résistance* of our trip, and we returned home without any further addition to the bag.

We had, however, seen a Skua and a Skua once seen is not a sight to be easily forgotten. There is a strange fascination about this dusky pirate of the sea—this tyrant who supports himself by levying toll on the hard-working Gulls and Terns. At first he may be observed preening his feathers on the sand unnoticing and unnoticed by the busy throng, and anon his sable form has swooped amongst the snow-white flock ; some shrieking bird is singled out as the victim, pursued with open beak, and forced to drop or disgorge its prey. The Skua seizes the fish, and all is quiet once more. Seen as I once saw it with a purple thunder-cloud for the background, and a pale green sea beneath, the spectacle is impressive in the extreme.

So a Skua became the object of our ambition ; in fact, with some members of the party, the pursuit of the Skua became little short of a mania. The birds seen on the Norfolk coast are mostly immature specimens of Richardson's Skua, though at times one of the rarer species is secured. I have twice seen the " Buffon " in the flesh ; both birds were light and speckled with grey, and they can be distinguished from the commoner species by the rounded tips of the two long tail feathers, and the fact that only the first two quills are white. We noticed—and we had good opportunities of doing so, for we spent hours at the bar in zealous but vain endeavours to get a shot—that the majority of the Richardsons, which varied in ground colour from light buff to dark brown, were to a certain extent albinos. They also seemed to fly within easy range of everybody except ourselves. On one occasion three of us waded into the water from opposite points and fairly enveloped a Skua while engaged in the pursuit of a Tern; but even then, when a shot seemed certain, it suddenly rose straight up and eluded us, the only result being a ducking for one of the trio who incautiously stepped into a submerged hole.

WAITING FOR THE TIDE.

We decided after this to give the boat another trial, and the following day saw us early *en route* for the bar. We bagged one or two Lapwings at the start, and then, passing the mud-flats without a stop, made straight for the estuary's mouth. As we turned the last corner, we espied in the distance the well-known form of the Skua, harrying as usual the flock of unoffending Terns. We were conscious also of a marked change coming over the movements of our boat; we were getting into rough water. We anchored, and it got still rougher as the wind rose, and the Skua showed no signs of coming within range. Proposals for a stroll along the shore became more and more frequent, and at length, when one bold spirit suggested lunch, B—— bluntly stated that he should enjoy his better on the land. Others seemed to think likewise, and the only one who actually did lunch in the boat was the boatman.

Meanwhile, the Skua gave up chasing Terns and took half an hour's aerial exercise in the rising gale. Never had I realized till then what his powers of flight were. At one moment he was buffeting with the wind on the far side of the estuary, and then with a single terrific swoop he had passed it, had left us in a twinkling, and was whirling with exultant sweeps across the sea. Our enjoyment of this flying exhibition was soon cut short by a shout from the boatman, who, fearful lest his boat should be carried out to sea, insisted on returning before the weather grew worse.

So the Skua had baffled us once more, and now it was our turn to take exercise—compulsory exercise of a very different sort—a hard row in the teeth of a stiff breeze and choppy sea. How we did get the boat round that corner goodness only knows; but this much is certain, there were wild words flying about, and much loss of temper—people half missing their stroke, and ladling sea-water over companions, or, worse still, companions' guns—a vision of rusted barrels and oily rags; and finally rain put the finishing touch to what everyone was now forced to recognize as a thoroughly disastrous day. We never thought about shooting till we were round the corner, and no shot was fired until we reached the home creek. Here in the gathering gloom someone had a bang at a Greenshank, declared that he had killed it, and condemned the rest of the party to a provoking and unprofitable search. We had indeed seen the reverse side of the picture, and it was with a feeling of general and undisguised relief that we at length came alongside of the lighter, and incontinently made tracks for the hotel.

As for the Skua, he mocked us once more on the morrow by flying over my head as I knelt with gun unloaded beside a wounded Wader. And the end was so prosaic after all ; a year later two of us met a dark specimen alone upon the sand, walked him up and shot him with ease. This is what most people do straight away, and our mismanagement of the business had been the joke of the village; but for all that, the Skua has become for us an historic bird, and stuffed in the oft seen attitude of pursuit after a Tern, it is, and always will be, one of the most highly prized ornaments of our museum.

Another bird that sometimes falls a victim to the man in the boat is the Heron. It is one of those creatures that you can often get close to when not over anxious to do so, and which on other occasions will hardly stay in the same parish. Walking along the Beaulieu River in the close season, I once followed a Heron for several miles. It retired into each creek before I got there, and flapped forth under my very nose when I arrived. But it is far otherwise in autumn on the mud-flats. Once only have I brought it to bag, and that was in a sailing boat drifting down before the gentlest of zephyrs, without the slighest expectation of a shot.   At two hundred yards the ever wakeful fisher looked up, stretched a wing, and treated us to a long, deliberate stare.   We all took it for granted that he was off; but no; by some unaccountable effort of avine reasoning he had persuaded himself that our intentions were harmless, and, calmly turning his back, devoted himself once more to the piscatorial art.   Inch by inch we drifted on, until, seeing that there was a chance after all, I borrowed the boatman's 8-bore—a weapon which I had always regarded with pious awe, but had never ventured to

AT THE BAR.

handle hitherto—and shortly afterwards letting fly with much trepidation, I was agreeably surprised to find my shoulder still intact, and the "Hanser" lying doubled up upon the sand.   That he would have let a mud-tramper come within range is improbable in the extreme, and his capture affords one of many instances of the subtle powers of self-insinuation possessed by a boat as opposed to a walking man.

Not that the boat can do much towards the acquisition of a specimen if the man doesn't do his share properly when the moment arrives, as I was made to realize very forcibly when pursuing two Great Crested Grebes in the following year.   Again the boat surpassed all expectations, and again, when we least expected it, we saw that we were in for a shot.   Though it was

c

September, one of these birds was in full breeding plumage and I was most eager to secure it.   We must have got within thirty yards, and I must confess I regarded it as to all intents and purposes my bird.   But I had been expecting it to dive, and when it rose instead and flew towards us I was so astonished that I stupidly blazed away both barrels while the Grebe was so close that I could see the red of its eye.   I suppose such misses have been made before, when the bird has been going one way and the boat the other, but at the time the thing seemed incredible; I could hardly believe that I had lost it.   My only consolation is the belief that, had I hit it at that distance, there would have been little left for anyone to stuff.

E. C. ARNOLD PINXT.]   A FAMILY PARTY.   (*Sheld-ducks.*)   [WEST NEWMAN.

CHAPTER IV.

FROM THE POINT OF VIEW OF A DUNLIN.

I BELONG to the ranks of the "inevitable" Dunlin, but I belong also to its small-beaked chestnut-coloured aristocracy, the inhabitants in spring time of the Yorkshire Fells. There are other members of our family—fat, country cousins, so to speak—who visit England in their thousands during migration without ever staying to breed in it; but we, the genuine Britishers, the Trojugenæ, if we may so style ourselves, look down upon them, and when we do meet in autumn on the shores, we keep ourselves apart from their motley gatherings on the mud-flats, and frequent rather the small tidal drains at the edge of the saltings, sometimes, though not often, consorting with our near relations the Little Stints.

It was late when I made my appearance on the Fells; the Grey Crows had robbed mother of her first clutch of eggs, and we were a second brood, but perhaps none the worse off on that account, since we escaped the drenching rain, which had killed off so many of our relatives in the early days of June. I remember admiring the beauty of the four egg-shells from which we had just emerged. The pale olive with its dark blotches shone beauteously in the morning sun, but mother and father soon made away with them, and then at once began to give us instructions in the art of feeding with one eye open and on the look-out for our constant enemies the birds of prey. Whenever any of us saw one of these in the distance, he gave the alarm in a low note, and we all crouched motionless amidst the tussocks until the marauder had passed out of sight. By great good fortune our family escaped unscathed, though two Merlins made sad havoc amongst some Titlarks which had just left their nests higher up upon the moor.

We now began to pay more attention to our dress and general appearance. Our dark brown coats of fluff, with their black and white speckling, compared, so we thought, most favourably with the more dingy colouring of our neighbours the young Lapwings, and as the quill feathers began to make their appearance on our wings, we spent much time in diligently pluming them during the long hours of the summer afternoon. Some allowance was perhaps to be made for this love of display in birds as young as we were, but father's vanity seemed even to us deplorable; he spent whole hours in preening and smoothing the bright black feathers of his waistcoat, and though mother did her best to excuse him by saying that when he lost this one he would have to go six months without another, we all thought he was becoming neglectful of his paternal duties, and one of my sisters finally said so outright, receiving in return a violent peck from father, which left a long ugly scar across her forehead, and only just missed injuring the eye itself.

One day in early August I had a terrible experience. Soon after midday two men appeared upon the moor accompanied by a dog. We had all heard of shooters, and been taught to dread them from our earliest days, and mother was in favour of instant flight. Father however declared that there was no need for alarm; the men had no guns with them, or we should have seen the barrels glistening, and in any case no shooting would be allowed at that time for fear of disturbing the grouse. They were only health-seekers come to the moors for exercise and fresh air. He followed up his remarks by volunteering to go and reconnoitre. Up he rose, and flew swiftly round them two or three times out of sheer bravado, and then came back to us with the news that there was nothing to fear.

"I don't like the look of that dog, my dear," said mother, as the three drew nearer to where we crouched; "if the men don't mean mischief, he does." And sure enough their spaniel had got wind of us and was rapidly approaching our retreat. We scuttled wildly; and father and mother, now fully alive to the danger, rose and flew with shrill cries round the heads of these intruders on our domain. As for me I lay half fascinated under a tuft of grass, and when I saw the monster's foam-flecked mouth drawing near me, and heard the fierce gasps that he emitted, I closed my eyes and gave myself up for lost. A moment later I was engulfed in a slimy chasm, where I lay too frightened to struggle or even to utter a squeak.

"Hallo! Jack, what's Shot got hold of? A young Dunlin, I believe. Here, Shot, drop it, dead," I heard a voice cry out above us, and then I was gently deposited on the ground, a hand closed over me and I was lifted up and curiously inspected by four gigantic eyes.

"What a pretty little chap," I heard, not without satisfaction, another voice remark; "but what a monstrous pair of feet he has; put him down and let us see him run."

Though not equally flattered by the last remark, I at once seized my opportunity and made tracks without delay to the nearest cover, the men meanwhile laughing heartily, and holding in the dog, which did its best to renew the chase.

"However did you escape?" asked my brother, as I lay panting but safe amidst my family.

"I don't know," I replied, faintly; for now that the excitement was over, I felt positively sick with fear.

It was not until near the end of August that father said it was time we left the Fells and began our journey southwards to our winter quarters; and before starting he gave us much advice concerning the dangers that we should have to encounter on the way. Most of our actual travelling was to be done by night, and having united with several other families that had bred upon the moor, we began to gradually work our way down the East coast. All went well until we reached the shore of Lincolnshire. It was misty weather when we got there, and many of our party flew into the long nets, which the fowlers here spread across the sand, and became entangled in their deadly meshes. We crossed the Wash by night in similar weather, and despite father's frequent calls it was a difficult matter to keep within touch of one another. All of a sudden a blaze of distant light appeared in the midst of the darkness, and by a common impulse our whole company made straight for this guiding torch; ignoring the warnings of several older birds—Terns, Waders, Chats, Swallows, Warblers—all fluttered madly towards the glare; but it went out suddenly even as it had appeared; we lost the line, and most of us passed just clear of a large stone erection, which I afterwards heard was a lighthouse. One of my sisters, indeed, who had judged the direction only too accurately, flew against its glass windows and fell a mangled corpse into the sea. Father said it was the revolving light that had saved us, and that in the old days when the lights were stationary many more used to be attracted to their doom.

And now we had reached a nice quiet estuary on the Norfolk coast, where father proposed to spend a week or so before proceeding further on our way. We scattered a bit as soon as it was light, and I passed the first morning snapping up small crustacea on some succulent ooze around an aged smack, that lay anchored in one of the most secluded creeks. Here I made the acquaintance of a small party of Turnstones, who pottered about amongst the stones and garbage not ten yards from the side of the smack. Two men were sitting on it, and I heard one of them say: "Well, Bob, what price your chicken to-morrow morning?"

I don't know why, but a queer sensation came over me, though I did not understand what he meant, and when I met father in the evening I told him what I had heard. He said he didn't like it: he was at all events glad he was not one of the Turnstones, and when mother said that she thought to-morrow must be the 1st of September, his look became still more serious, and, gathering the whole family together, he proceeded to give us what he said might prove useful information.

"To-morrow," he began, "will come the shooters, and it will be a dangerous day for all of us. Still we Dunlins need not be so much afraid as some. We are neither large enough nor toothsome enough to provide a meal for the pot-hunter, who, though he may rake a flock of our larger and more numerous cousins with an eye to a pie, will hardly think us worth a cartridge, if we rise singly. We have most to dread from schoolboys out for the first time, and from the collectors—I mean the more dull-visioned collectors; there are many who shoot at all single waders in the hope of getting an American stray, and we, being smaller and brighter than ordinary Dunlins, may be easily mistaken for something rare. I advise you if you do get cornered by a collector—you can generally tell them by their field-glasses—to rise quite slowly, and utter our note as distinctly and as soon as you can; their ears may be better than their eyes, and the note may save you. As for schoolboys, heaven help you! if you meet any of them. Two of them pursued my wife last year with such inconsiderate ardour, that when they fired, the greater portion of the charge, after missing her, fairly smothered a collector, who was coming the other way. Poor fellow! After the dose he went and sat down for nearly half-an-hour on a buoy to recover his senses, and then limped painfully home; I felt quite sorry for him. But above all things keep clear of the professor; neither note nor plumage will avail you there. Did he not in one day slaughter eighty Redstarts in the hope of killing a Bluethroat amongst them?"

This sort of talk was not such as to make one look forward to the morrow, and I think we all passed a somewhat agitated night. I dreamt about that poor collector that the boys potted, and wondered how it felt. Long before sunrise I was awake, and drawn by some irresistible attraction I made my way to the smack to have a look at my friends the Turnstones. There they were, quite a dozen of them, just awakening from their slumbers and preparing to get their breakfast among the stones. The sun rose, and shortly afterwards a commotion was observable on the smack, and mindful of father's warning I flew off at once to a more distant bank, vainly trying to warn the Turnstones as I did so. From here I watched six figures carrying guns, and one bearing a sack, creep cautiously off the boat and steal towards the unsuspecting flock. Bang! bang! again and again went the guns; the work of destruction had begun. Six out of the dozen already lay dead or dying on the sand; four more shared the same fate as they flew wildly round the slain.

The two survivors flew shrieking over my head. For a moment I was too horrified to move.

"Not bad that for a start," said one of the butchers; and then, while the man with the sack gathered up the victims, he began advancing towards the bank on which I crouched. Remembering that I was not worth a cartridge, I rose with a confident "peep." Bang! bang! went the gun on an instant; a hail of shots swept by me. Three of my long pinions were cut in two; a toe was severed from my right foot, and a third shot whizzed through the feathers of my breast. Still no vital spot was touched, and I tore away amidst the curses of the shooter and the derisive laughter of his friends.

What could father have been thinking of? These men spare anything? Not they! They were shooting neither for the pot nor the cabinet; their aim was a colossal bag! And now from a distant sandbank I watched them form in long line across the estuary. Off they started, driving all the birds before them in a terrified and frantic mob. No living thing came amiss to their sportsmanship. Terns, Redshanks, Turnstones, Knots, Plovers, Dunlins, one after the other sank into the mud. A sheep feeding at the edge of the saltings received a pellet through the fleshy part of its nose; an old mussel-seeker similarly peppered in the lumbar regions, as he bent over his work, straightened himself with language that would have made a self-respecting Dunlin blush; a man on board a tug, who ventured to remonstrate, was told that he himself would be the next victim if he didn't go below. He went and he stayed there! *Quid enim facis cum furiosus cogit et idem fortior?* The end came at length; the place became a wilderness, hardly a bird in the same parish, and these few as wild as Hawks. The butchers counted up their bag, one hundred and thirty odd—whether rare or common they knew not, neither did they care; they had broken their record. They left the estuary; they could sleep the sleep of the just.

I did not expect to see any of my family again after that dreadful day, but our liking for outlying drains and pools had proved our salvation; we had just kept clear of their beat, and we gathered together in the evening and sorrowfully discussed the events of the day. Odd guns now frequented the mudflats every morning, but, as father had prophesied, we single Dunlin seemed to be contemned by all. Once I was surprised by a shooter with glasses, and had to rise in front of him. He was going to fire, but fortunately I remembered father's advice, and just got out a hurried "peep" in time. The gun was lowered, and feeling that I was being examined through the glasses, I flew slowly so as to give a full view of my plumage. The collector at last turned his back. Thank goodness, he was satisfied—and so was I.

That evening we assembled for the last time as a family. I thought father looked rather worried. He did not seem as proud as usual of his black waistcoat; in fact, he said he thought some collector was after him on that account. Poor father! he was right. The very next day he heard a brother Dunlin calling from a white object floating in the estuary. Fond as ever of society, he flew up gaily to make the new-comer's acquaintance. Twenty yards off; alas! too late he recognised the fraud. The white object was a boat, the call was being uttered by a boatman, and it was the wily collector who greeted him with a dose of No. 8, and, as he carefully retrieved his body from the water, remarked to his companion: "A good black-breaster for September; just beginning to moult his quill feathers; I expect it's the one I was pursuing the best part of yesterday afternoon."

My brother too had a desperately near shave on the same day. He had been pursued by a Peregrine, which missed him by an inch, as he skimmed across the water, so violent being the stoop of the great bird that it was itself for the time being almost totally submerged.

Mother said that if we had to keep our eyes open for the Peregrine as well as the shooters, life would not be worth living in the estuary. So we decided to move on to warmer and less frequented abodes. Here we changed our dress to a duller grey, and uniting with the remnants of other families formed a huge flock, which except in very severe weather was almost unapproachable by our foes.

When spring appeared I began to grow a black waistcoat myself, and became possessed at the same time of a desire to return to my native fells. We set out in small parties of half a dozen, the journey being far less dangerous than in the autumn. We were all strong of wing, the weather was fine, and there were no shooters, and though one or two of our party lost their lives by flying against telegraph wires, yet the bulk of us reached our breeding ground in safety; and here I am just considering which young lady I shall pay court to. But first let me see what these two men mean by intruding on our preserves. Men don't carry guns at this season, and if they did, I remember father said they dare not use them, so I may as well go and have a good look at that very ancient Norfolk jacket that one of them is wearing. Ah! they seem to be admiring my black waistcoat. One of them lifts a spy-glass to observe it better. *O Chrysaetos!*

CHAPTER V.

SOUTH CORNWALL.

THE lodestone which attracted me to South Cornwall was Marazion Marsh, and on Marazion Marsh I saw one Dunlin, and never fired a shot. It was easy, nevertheless, to picture to oneself American Waders disporting themselves amidst its reeds and tussocks in a previous age. The books ascribe to it a Yellowshank and a Solitary Sandpiper at least, and it may well, thanks mainly to its geographical position, have produced other rarities of a similar type, but like most of these historic hunting grounds the place must have sadly changed since those palmy days. Now a railroad runs through its midst; it is getting gradually drained, and the surviving pools are few in number, and not particular promising. Lastly, it is in private hands, and, though one might perhaps have got leave to shoot over it by asking, the neighbouring foreshore between Penzance and St. Michael's Mount seemed, at all events in August, to be the more likely locality of the two. Here I passed several mornings in a careful examination of the flocks of smaller Waders that frequented it, and, as shooting is allowed in Cornwall during the above-mentioned month, there was an unusual chance of getting summer plumaged specimens of the commoner birds. Black-breasted Dunlins were plentiful, and Sanderlings were scattered amongst them also in their summer dress.

On the 6th of August I came across three beautiful Turnstones, and on the following day a pair of Oystercatchers added further variety to the scene. Ringed Plover were very numerous and tame, but, though I turned my glasses on nearly every bird in the hope of an American stray, I never came across anything that looked the least suspicious. Great excitement was occasioned one morning amongst these Waders by the sudden advent of a Peregrine, but, though his sombre form created a regular panic as it glided by, he took, so far as I could see, no notice of the scurrying flocks, but passed straight out to sea without doing harm to anything.

After firing one shot in three days, I paid a flying visit to the Land's End. We walked from the Logan Rock to the hotel in the hope of seeing a large

Hawk or a Raven, but nothing appeared more exciting than a Kestrel, though at the Land's End itself Shags and Cormorants were numerous, and it was interesting to see Wild Herring Gulls feeding side by side with domestic fowls. A stay of a week on the Lizard promontory was far more entertaining from an ornithological point of view. The country here is much wilder, and the cliff scenery more attractive to birds. We began by exploring the Goonhill Downs as being a recognized resort of Harriers. They were certainly wild enough and well suited to their habits in other ways, but all we actually saw was a Crake of some sort disappearing into reeds, and various Kestrels suspended over the moor.

On returning to the Lizard, we called at the cottage of the local naturalist, where we saw a stuffed Peregrine and a Chough, both killed some years before, and learnt that a Harrier had been slain in the preceding spring by a farmer, who waited a fortnight for the shot. So much for the chance of meeting with one of these birds nowadays, even in their most favoured haunts! As for the Chough, it was seven years since one had been seen. Peregrines were not so scarce. Twice, at least, my brother got a glimpse of this bird while bathing before breakfast, and on one occasion two were playing with one another in mid-air near the Lizard Lighthouse.

But perhaps the most characteristic bird of the neighbourhood was the Raven. We only realised just before leaving that it was as common as it was. True, the old fisherman asserted that he could find one any time upon the cliffs, and so no doubt he could. I, myself, in pursuance of the programme sketched out by him, spent a whole day between the Lizard and Kynance vainly endeavouring to outwit what proved after all to be nothing more than a pair of Carrion Crows. I can claim little credit for the discovery, which was not even due to my own powers of observation, but came about in this way.

Towards evening, I was for the twentieth time, or thereabouts, proceeding to try and stalk a sable figure perched upon a projecting rock of wide prospect. Judged in the light of various similar attempts, it was likely to prove a futile undertaking, but whatever slight chances of success I may have possessed were suddenly extinguished by a wild halloo from the cliff above. The bird decamped in a twinkling, and in no very amiable frame of mind I turned to seek the author of the shout. It was a queer sight that I beheld—a ragged, uncouth figure was carelessly descending the cliff with a peculiar rolling gait that threatened each minute to hurl him forward down the slope, fortunately not a very steep one at this spot. As he drew near I perceived that, though not exactly drunk, he was at all events in the state nautically known as "half seas over," and I advanced at once from the edge in order to prevent him from approaching it. To my relief he seemed well disposed, and having introduced himself as "only a bit of a moucher, that did no harm to anybody, but just had a few rabbit snares down below," he went on to suggest that I should have a shot at a rabbit myself. I explained that I was after a Raven, and as my late quarry was still within sight, I signified my intention of pursuing it.

"That a Ra-aven," said the moucher, with ill-concealed disdain; "why, it's a Crow!" And as six others turned up at this moment and joined company with my bird, I saw at once that he was right. Not a little humbled by this rebuff, I asked if he knew where the Ravens were, and made out at length, from his somewhat disconnected utterances, that they came very early every morning to a certain butcher's refuse heap within a quarter of a mile of Lizard Town. I then left him to his rabbits, and the Crow to its well-earned repose, returned forthwith to my lodgings, and arranged to be called next morning at five o'clock. The field I knew well, having previously marked it as a likely place, for I had seen both Crows and Gulls hovering over it as we drove in the first afternoon. It was within range of two low walls, and seemed in every way suitable for a successful stalk.

Alas! for human calculations; the refuse heap, a veritable bovine golgotha, was *too* attractive. Birds were always coming and going, and it was moreover too near the high-road. As we approached, a Crow arose and hovered. It saw us, and giving the alarm put up every bird in the field, and away they went, the Ravens, if there were any, with them. The only thing to do was to retire to the village and give them time to settle again. Half an hour later we again advanced to the assault, crawled across the first field, and reached the cover of the wall. Rising cautiously behind some furze bushes, we got a partial view of the refuse heap, on the top of which stood a grand old Greater Black-backed Gull. Around were a number of Herring-Gulls and Crows, and while we peered about to try and discover a Raven, they gradually got wind of our presence, and before we had completed our inspection up they got in a confused mass. We both fired hurriedly at the Black-back, but to our intense disgust away he sailed apparently untouched, and two wretched immature Herring Gulls fell headlong to the ground. Such was the end of our first attempt. The second was equally exasperating. On the next day we again got up early and set off for the heap. While still on the road, a man passed us in a cart, and his horse saw fit to jib just opposite the Raven's field. The noise of the ensuing altercation put up everything before we could get within range, and we had the pleasure of hearing the undoubted croak of a Raven amidst the departing crowd. The next day was our last, and once more we were doomed to failure. We got there too early this time, and a couple of Ravens coming up from behind as we were crawling across the field, saw us, gave one croak apiece, and flew straight back to the sea.

The best portion of the cliffs for sea fowl was that around Kynance Cove. Herring Gulls and Lesser Black-backs bred plentifully on an insulated rock shut off from the main-land by a deep but narrow gorge, and from the rocks on the land side one could watch in comfort the domestic life of its inhabitants. Straight opposite, a Shag flew out from a nest with young, the naked, sooty forms of the nestlings being plainly visible across the dividing chasm. Higher up towards the summit of the rock there was a strip of crumbling soil, which was much affected by the youthful Gulls. Several had left the nest, but were as yet unable to fly, and they hunched about in true Gull fashion, uttering a persistent and dismal whistle as they did so, while others practised the art of flying by leaping downwards from rock to rock. Once I became the witness of a tug of war between two of their parents. A bird had just arrived with a fish in its beak, which it was preparing to distribute to its young. Suddenly another Gull, either a pirate by nature, or one whose moral sense was undermined by the arduous task of supporting so voracious a family, saw a short way to providing them with a meal. As the triumphant fisher passed, it shot forth its beak and laid firmly hold of the projecting portion of the fish. The struggle that ensued was very different to what I expected. There were no wild jerks or side rushes. The combatants solemnly secured a reliable foot-hold, and then proceeded to settle matters by a steady pull. I regret now that I did not time them from the start, for the tug must have lasted two minutes at the least. At times, by mutual consent, they seemed to relax the strain and secure fresh footholds, and then they went grimly on, apparently unnoticed by the other Gulls. The finish was, I must confess, rather tame—one of them, the would-be robber, gave up quite suddenly without any final effort that I could see, and without making any attempt to secure a fresh hold of the fish, which the victor then distributed without further molestation to its young.

Towards evening the Gulls from the inland fields would flight over the cliffs to the island in a steady stream, and anyone who hid behind one of the numerous scattered boulders could easily get a specimen of an adult Herring Gull, but the Black-backs were much more wary, and for the most part kept well out to sea. We badly wanted a Shag, and as the sea was too rough for a visit to the Stag Rocks, which are crowded with them, our only chance was to get one at Kynance Cove. On the last evening we went there, having previously noticed that the birds are given to circling round the so-called Asparagus Island. This picturesque rock is even at high tide united to the mainland by a strip of sand. When we commenced operations it was about ten yards broad, and as no boat could be got, the idea was to try and drop one on this strip, as they ran or rather flew the gauntlet between the island and the mainland. We sat down half way up the cliff and watched the Shags fishing or preening themselves on an adjacent rock, some of the attitudes they adopted being quite unlike anything I had ever seen in a book. One came and swam right under us in typical waterlogged style, and we might perhaps have shot it, but refrained from doing so, as the body would have drifted out to sea.

At length, as the evening wore on, a spirit of unrest came over the whole company. They took wing, singly and in pairs, and began flying round the island. Several came towards us and appeared certain to cross the fatal strip, but they always swerved off before they got within shot, though they had passed readily enough on the previous day when we had no guns. While we wondered at their refusal to pass us, a peal of laughter from the top of the cliff revealed the fact that we were not its only occupants. A picnic party was just breaking up and starting off for its char-a-banc. We also bethought us, that though better sheltered, we were a shade lower down than on the preceding day, and, as the sun was now sinking, we hurried off to the top of the cliff. Though little time remained, and the birds were beginning to settle down for the night, we were destined to get a shot after all. Just as we were departing, a single bird arose, whirled high once or twice round the top of the island, and then made a sudden dash for the gully. It came through at a terrific pace, but we both managed to fire while it was above the strip. There was a wild stagger, and I thought for the moment it was down, but unfortunately it just recovered itself and, skimming away on a rapidly declining course, it succeeded in rounding the island, and fell heavily some distance out at sea.

It was too dark now to hope for any further shots, and we had to abandon all hopes of getting a Shag during our visit. The Cormorant is almost equally common along this coast, and at Mullion, on an outlying island, there is a Puffin colony, while at the pretty little village of Cadgwith the Kittiwake is numerous and absurdly tame, sitting quietly on the lowest rocks while the boats pass close to it on their way into the cove. In winter Golden Plover are said to be plentiful on the moors, and also Duck; but past experience of the value of local statements on such subjects would make me chary in these days of going bail for the appearance of any species of the Anatidæ.

CHAPTER VI.

THE BROADS.

THE ancient reputation of the Broads, coupled with the fascination of their seductive scenery, and even the mere fact that they are practically the sole resort of the Bearded Tit, will always induce naturalists to visit them; it is only a question of *when* their magnetic influence will exert its power. But, supposing that we do set out for this El Dorado of the ornithologist's imagination, what are we likely to meet with when we get there?

Now, I lay no claim to any intimate acquaintance with the bird life of East Anglia. People who live in this district have regaled us with descriptions of the splendid sights to be seen there. We read of five Harriers seen on the wing in a single day, and within a short distance of whole families of Crested Grebes and Bearded Tits; and we get hints of even Ruffs still sparring and nesting in the more sequestered spots. And no one doubts the truth of these stories; only they describe the privileges that belong not to the many, but to the few—the few who dwell upon the spot. The many go to the Broads only at intervals, and for a short time; and the following record of what I myself have met with in various sporadic expeditions may be taken by such intending visitors as giving a rough but fairly accurate idea of what they themselves are likely to encounter if they go there as strangers, without any credentials to admit them to the private and more secluded Broads.

Probably no one will be under the delusion that he will be able to shoot. There is no free shooting in Broadland, save on Breydon Water, and of that free shooting more anon. For an ordinary visit, one must abandon the gun for the field-glasses. As regards the choice of seasons, I should vote without hesitation for the spring or early summer, for to the explorer of these lagoons a calm day is the first essential; a stiff wind ruins everything.

My earliest pilgrimage dates back to June, 1889, when, in company with a fellow undergraduate, equally keen on natural history, I paid a flying visit from Cambridge to Wroxham and Salhouse Broads. I must confess to having been rather taken aback. The fine reed-fringed expanse of Wroxham was indeed much what I had pictured it, but I had expected to find the Broads

E. C. ARNOLD PINXT.]

[WEST NEWMAN.

THE PRIZE FOR VALOUR. (*Ruffs and Reeve.*)

THE BROADS.

connected with one another by marshy tracts of waste land, and found, instead, green fields running right up to the edge. We had an interesting day, nevertheless. As we sculled in from the river, we put up a wild Duck, disembarked, and walked straight up to the nest, and then, drifting out on to the glassy waters of the Broad, found ourselves before long intent on watching the motions of a pair of Great Crested Grebes, resplendent in all the glories of the breeding plumage. They at least came up to my expectations, and we sat and watched them for nearly an hour. They did not seem wild, but remained persistently about eighty yards off, diving at once if we attempted to get nearer, but regarding us rather as intruders than as dangerous enemies to be escaped. I have no doubt now that they were nesting; but in those days I hardly knew a Grebe's nest from a Moorhen's, and the casual search in which we indulged was based on totally wrong principles to begin with. Later in the day we moved on to Salhouse, and, forcing our skiff along a narrow channel, where the oars were useless, and the only method of progression was by pulling at the bushes on either side, we at length invaded the sanctity of a small private Broad. Here M—— had seen a Bearded Tit in the preceding spring, but on this occasion we failed to find one after a two hours' search. It was a delightful nook all the same; less than half an acre in extent, and nestling within a belt of the densest reeds, its still brown waters carpeted in parts with lilies, and dotted with miniature islands of rank, luxuriant vegetation, it was an ideal piece of Broadland, a scene of absolute peace and seclusion. The Coots and Moorhens might just have come forth from the Ark, so tame were they. Their nests met us at every turn, and the birds themselves, their dark forms faintly mirrored on the placid surface of the mere, paddled all around us amid the water-plants, utterly fearless of the boat's approach.

Some days later we organised a picnic to Scoulton Mere, and, setting forth in two large punts, with several ladies, spent the day in punting round the swampy island which shelters the colony of Lesser Black-headed Gulls. The social conviviality of a picnic party being hardly conducive to ornithological research, the only find was a Reed Warbler's nest. But our visit to the Gulls' nesting-place proved most interesting to everyone. As we approached, the whole company of sitting birds arose, and in one white cloud hovered shrieking above our heads. When we landed, the oft-told story, that it was difficult to avoid treading on their eggs, proved, to our astonishment, literally true; there were hundreds of nests within quite a small radius. We were neatly ambushed by a watcher while engaged in annexing a few eggs, but after much persuasion he was at length induced to allow us to keep three as a memento of the visit. One of these was a very interesting specimen, the ground colour being light blue. We could not discover that the Shoveller was breeding, though I believe it has done so since, nor could we find any traces of the Bearded Tit.

Ten years later, chance bringing me within reach of Yarmouth, I decided to pay a visit to the more Eastern Broads. Breydon was to be the centre of attraction, and we reached Yarmouth on September 10th. Ill fortune dogged us from the start. While putting our guns together after breakfast, something went wrong with one of F——'s triggers, and it was arranged that he should proceed to the nearest gunsmith's, while we chartered a boat for the day. The boathouses were said to be close at hand, and we started forth under the guidance of the " boots." Some boathouses were close by, but they had no available boats, and we wandered on for a considerable distance through crooked lanes and alleys before we at last secured a suitable craft. We then sent the " boots " back to the hotel to bring up the missing gun, but the latter, who had returned earlier than was expected, and had grown tired of waiting, had started forth to track us on his own account, and by the time he was retrieved from the above-mentioned network of alleys, we were informed that we had missed the proper tide. Forth we went nevertheless, and, mingling at first in the stream of wherries, pleasure steamers and barges, got through the stone bridge with some difficulty, and found ourselves at length on the " Queen of the Broads."

What sort of sport Breydon may be able to afford on occasions, I am unable to say. Doubtless its geographical position, and its vast muds, almost too vast in places, attract rarities at times; and when there is a migration on, there may even be good shooting if the tide is right. For us the tide was wrong, there was no migration on, and no rarities were present, and the shooting was positively nil; three guns between them never fired a shot. A quarter of a mile from the bridge we might, had we chosen, have raked a small flock of Dunlin, and by the look on our boatman's face when we didn't fire, we guessed that he had no expectation of meeting many birds beyond. These Dunlin had already run the gauntlet of another boatful, and left one of their number winged upon the muds, and the whole party were now standing up having shots at it, one after the other, without any apparent effect. After the fusillade had lasted several minutes, and as the bird seemed none the worse, the boatman was at length instructed to take off his boots, and run it down on the muds. This he did, though with no effusive readiness, while we lay by and watched the whole performance; it was the most exciting episode of the day. We then stuck all but permanently on the mud, and, when we did get off, it was decided that we should land and walk along the sea-wall, while the man worked his way through a shallow channel and met us higher up. Near the wall we found a winged Redshank, which formed the day's total bag, and, rejoining the boat soon afterwards, we spent the next few hours lying across the main channel in the hope of a stray shot, and listening to stories of Spoonbills, &c., shot by Booth and other well-known collectors. Not a bird came within range, and though we had powerful glasses and scanned the muds in all directions, the only winged creatures that we could see were a few Heron, a fair sprinkling of Gulls (all Lesser Black-headed), one or two odd Curlew, and a single Whimbrel which we might conceivably have stalked. After that first flock of Dunlin, we never saw another small Wader throughout the day. The boatman at length proposed working the channels, and, determined to give the place a fair trial, we consented, and solemnly journeyed along each without the slightest hope of a shot. Nothing upset our calculations; not a bird was to be found. To while away the time I took a few photographs, none of which ever came out, and then, as there were obvious signs of an approaching deluge, we set to and rowed hard for home. We did escape the rain, and it was about the only thing we did do successfully on that ill-fated day.

I doubt whether I shall ever visit Breydon again ; not that I consider it a bad place, despite our experience. The fact is, that anyone living on the spot, and able to go out as soon as birds have arrived, would no doubt have excellent sport at times, but it is not worth going there at random on the chance of finding birds. They evidently use it as a resting-place rather than a haunt.

On the following day we took the train to Potter Heigham with the idea of searching for Bearded Tits on Hickling Broad, but again the Fates were against us. Passing the Falgate, the inn well known as the headquarters of the late Mr. E. T. Booth, we soon got down to the river, and here at one time we seemed likely to spend the day. The place swarmed with boats and boat-houses, but of a boatman we could see no signs. After an irritating wait of half an hour, we unearthed one of the boat proprietors, and by his persuasion a boatman, so called, was extracted from a neighbouring inn.

"Did he know anything about the birds of the neighbourhood?" we enquired rather anxiously, after a hurried scrutiny of our would-be guide. His knowledge was explained to be unimpeachable, and though this was more than could be said for his appearance—he reeked of beer—for want of anyone better we reluctantly engaged him and got into the boat. We suggested that one of us should scull while he steered, but this he would not hear of, and as it did not seem politic to offend him, after fervently thanking our stars that we could swim, we sat grimly down and waited developments. They were not long in coming. We had to get through the stone arches of the bridge which

D

here spans the river, and it proved a stupendous undertaking, it being doubtful at one time whether the passage was to be negotiated with the bows or stern in front, and our final success was owing less to the efforts of the oarsman than to the manual exertion of B——, who was seated in the bows, and who, by painfully clawing the rough stonework, contrived after a time to pull us through. Several yachts, a·wherry, and an odd boat or two lay on the far side, and after Providence had worried us a way through these, not without much extraneous vituperation, we emerged at length on the open waters of the Thurne.

We had so far deferred all questions as to the haunts of the birds, but now someone ventured to ask where he expected to find the Tits. The answer was slow in coming, but monumental when it arrived : as the sun was shining, he anticipated that they would be " lying at the bottoms of the pools beneath the reeds ! "

It did not strike us as a likely domicile, but we abstained from criticism, and sat still in gloomy silence until at a fork in the river our boat came to a sudden stop. Our Charon was evidently hazy as to the route, and tried to solve the difficulty by volunteering to take us to both Hickling and Horsey during the day. We said that one, if it was Hickling, would satisfy us, and as a fishing boat fortunately turned up at this critical moment, we got directions from those on board, and were soon again in motion towards Heigham Sound. Here a strongish wind arose, and the rough water proving too much for Charon's dubious watermanship, he was at length induced to relinquish the sculls. Not long afterwards he was tenderly laid to rest in the bows, where he snored contentedly for the remainder of the day.

Left to our own resources, we pulled steadily on along the Sound, turning aside at times to explore some of the small pools which occur now and then amidst the forest of reeds which border them. Here B——, anxious to exhibit his skill as a punter, recently acquired as it was by various watery experiences at Oxford, volunteered to give us. an exhibition for variety's sake, and I am bound to say quanting proved far the most effective method of getting about. As for the Reed Pheasants, carefully though we looked for them, we could find no trace of their presence, though it is just possible that we heard their note once—or, to be more accurate, a sound which we did hear might, by a slight stretch of imagination, have been described as representing the " ping, ping " of the bird books.

We were, however, most unlucky in the weather ; the wind got worse, and the sun went in, and I should imagine it was just the sort of afternoon on which they would skulk at the bottoms of the reeds. Goodness only knows whether

MARSH HARRIER.

E. C. ARNOLD DEL.] [WEST NEWMAN.

we did, or didn't, get to Hickling. We reached an open piece of water, with stakes across it, and thought at the time that we were there. Subsequent investigation, however, threw some doubts on the truth of this belief, and the disputed question still remains unsolved.

We actually saw, during that day on the Broads, one Curlew, two Terns (probably Common), one Heron, one Moorhen, and Coots *ad lib*. We also heard the note of the Redshank once.

Although everything comes to him that waits, even a Bearded Tit, it was not until five years later that I at last made the expedition which saw me return from Broadland a really contented man. I had, after a solemn promise that I would reveal the locality to no one, got leave to visit a private Broad, which was said to be frequented by the Bearded Tit, and the day that resulted surpassed my highest hopes : I then saw Broadland at its best. With my two brothers and S——, a volunteer captain possessed of an appropriate knowledge of firearms, I arrived about ten o'clock at the little village of X——. Here our guide met us, and we were soon stowed away in a flat-bottomed punt, and being steadily propelled towards the Broad. We had understood that the Tits were to be shot from a boat, and had therefore come by train, dressed in ordinary clothes, and it was rather disconcerting to discover, as we went along, that the spot where the birds were to be met with was not on a Broad at all, but on an undrained marsh close to it, where there were " some dry spots here and there." With a silent prayer that the Tits might see fit to visit one of these, we settled down to enjoy the beauties of the row. It was a lovely morning, with the sun shining brightly, and without a breath of wind, and we felt confident that, so far as weather went, we had stumbled on an ideal day. The route lay through a forest of reeds and water-plants, among which the most characteristic were the water-lilies, while a confiding Kingfisher accompanied us almost from the start. Coots and Moorhens also abounded, and the note of the Sedge Warbler resounded incessantly from the banks. Where these were clear of foliage, we gazed upon swampy marshes, which reminded me most of Wicken Fen ; it was the wildest portion of the Broads that I had ever been to. And now our boatman, whom I shall call —— in future, turned aside from the main stream, and running the punt into a narrow dyke signified that it was time to disembark. My eye lighted at once on a large Raptorial hovering over a distant portion of the marsh, and Z—— asserted that it was a Harrier. We accepted it as a good omen, and stepped forth on to a raised bank. Hardly had we done so, when a harsh note resounded from the very dyke we had entered, and it needed no Broadsman to tell us that it was the note of the bird we sought. I should have rendered it

D 2

"chang" rather than "ping" myself. In a moment all was excitement; Z——, who was a grand old fellow, being as keen as anyone. Posting us a few yards apart along the bank, he assured us that the birds would soon climb to the tops of the reeds. It looked as if we were going to get them dryshod after all. The reeds, however, were very dense, being a mixture of reeds proper, rushes, and sedge, and though the old hand caught occasional glimpses of a bird, we novices could never succeed in locating one. Thus we waited for the best part of half an hour, and there seemed every probability of our continuing to wait; not one came actually to the top. We now arranged a drive. Z—— was to advance along the dyke in his waders, while we stood two on each side at its end. We had promised on no account to fire back, the idea being that the birds would fly between us towards the open ground beyond.

We were to permit them to reach it, and then anyone could let drive. As Z—— advanced, we heard the Tits' scolding note preceding him along the dyke, and noticing, as I did, the obvious excitement of the others, I began to feel that the drive was likely to prove as dangerous to us as to the birds. The same idea occurred simultaneously to S——, who, after backing uneasily for several yards, a manœuvre which brought me into his line of fire, saw fit to enter a protest just at the moment when the Tits reached the end of the dyke. They took the hint, and rising barely clear of the reeds doubled straight back over the driver's head, subsequently wheeling into a large reed bed on the left. As they flew, they uttered another note. It was doubtless that which has been likened by Stevenson to the clashing of cymbals, for we thought it sounded very musical. After liberal free criticism of one another's conduct and of the arrangements for the drive, we took up a fresh position, and Z—— once more entered the reeds. It was a more open bed than the last, and soon we saw him signalling that he could actually see the birds. His keenness was infectious; abandoning cat-like principles, I pulled up my trousers above the knee, and, resolved to sacrifice boots, socks, and pants, and chance what might result from the journey back, I rushed into the water, and quickly found myself at Z——'s side. The birds meantime had disappeared again, but, having once taken the plunge, I tramped after them, put up an old cock right under my nose, and knocked him over just as he showed signs of dropping again. I had doubts whether we should retrieve him at first, but I kept my eye fixed on the spot where he fell, and at last found him floating among the stalks. We knew there were other birds about from the drive, and it was not long before I flushed a hen. The reeds here were as high as my head, and thinking she was dropping, I fired too hurriedly and missed her clean. She then pitched in a dry patch, and G. F. joined me for the next attempt, while

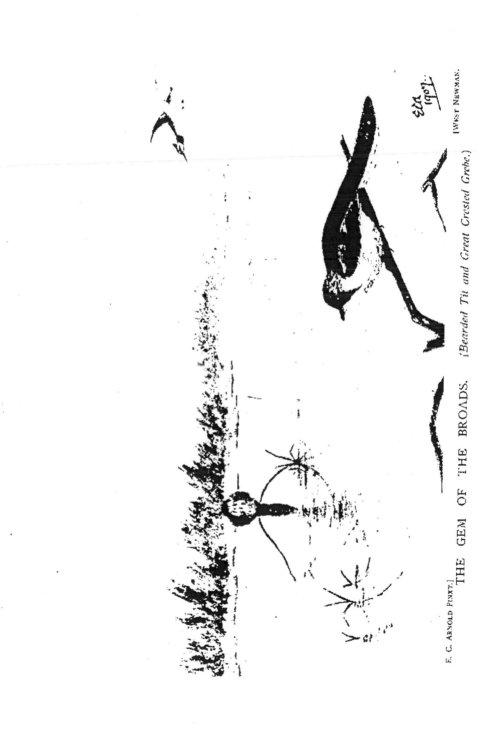

F. C. ARNOLD PINXT.]   THE GEM OF THE BROADS.   (*Bearded Tit and Great Crested Grebe.*)

[WEST NEWMAN.

R. B. stood handy with a walking-stick gun prepared to wipe the eye of either or both. He never got the chance, for she fell to an easy shot before she reached him. We now adjourned to lunch, at which my strange costume, the most prominent feature of which was a pair of pants soaked brown to the middle of the calves, provoked much merriment, until someone discovered that, owing to a servant's error, soap and water was the only beverage contained in our flasks.

Thus refreshed, and with our interest stimulated anew by Z——'s statement that there was a small Warbler somewhere on the marsh different to any he had ever seen before, we determined to enter a part where the vegetation was thicker still. I stuck to my costume as being incapable of further depreciation, but S—— thought to improve upon it by entering in boots, but with bare legs; it may be said at once that this was a failure. Cut by the sedge, and stung by various insects, his calves next day presented the appearance of balloons, and, while we were shooting, he was lying on the sofa wrestling with an incipient attack of blood poisoning, which he only just succeeded in warding off.

But to return to the Broads. I had hopes from Z——'s description that the Warbler mentioned might turn out an Aquatic, and I knocked over two suspicious creatures that we put out. These birds, though they proved only to be Sedge Warblers, gave us an opportunity of admiring Z——'s extraordinary powers as a retriever. When the first bird fell in what appeared a hopeless jungle, he never despaired for a moment, but quickly set to work to trace the passage of the shot. This he did by looking for shot holes and tears in the reeds; later on he found a feather, then a fleck of blood, and finally the bird itself was brought to light. His tracking powers were worthy of a Red Indian, and when the second bird fell in a place little less difficult we were all quite prepared to see it found. While resting from our exertions for a few moments, we got a distant view of what Z—— called a "Game-Hawk." I could not identify it myself at the distance, but I gathered from his description that it was a Peregrine. As time went on, the prospect of an hour's railway journey in soaked boots grew less and less enticing, and when Z—— suggested that we should go to his home, get tea, and endeavour to dry ourselves, everyone jumped at the proposal. The visit was a great success, and I have seldom enjoyed a tea more than the one set before us in this snug little cottage. We sat with our feet in blankets while our boots and socks were being baked in the kitchen oven, the end of it being that we returned dry-shod in the evening, possessed at last of some Bearded Tits, and having spent a thoroughly delightful day.

Afterwards, while I was stuffing the birds, we had a random discussion on the position of the Bearded Tit in ornithology. S——, who knew least on the subject, laid it down that it was most nearly allied to the Bullfinch! The rest agreed that the local name of Reed Pheasant was more satisfactory than Bearded Tit. I saw myself no similarity to a Tit in any of their actions, whereas their appearance as they rose was rather suggestive of a small Pheasant. When it came to skinning them, apart from the shape of the tail, I noticed a certain resemblance in the texture of the feathers to those of the Dartford Warbler, and, as in the case of the latter bird, there is a sort of sturdiness about them; one is not surprised that they can brave the rigours of our English cold. They seemed always to be in the thickest part of the reeds, where there was water beneath them, and, when once alarmed, nothing short of trampling would get them out, and when they were out one had to shoot quickly, or they were in again, and this makes it very difficult to get a good specimen for stuffing. I doubt whether they are as rare as they are said to be. We heard the note several times after we had got our birds, and Z—— said that he could get a pair whenever he wanted them, but he was fully cognisant of their charms, and never shot them himself. He said that in the spring they often came and sat quite close to him as he worked on his marsh.

CHAPTER VII.

FLIGHTING.

PEOPLE more often go "flighting" than "flight-shooting," and this is especially true of the stranger who sets forth to bag the vespertinal Duck upon the saltings. And yet, though birds do so often follow a regular line of flight, I would myself far sooner go after them unattended by the local professional, who already knows that line. Half the fun, I think, lies in endeavouring to discover it for yourself.

To pit one's own prescience against that of several friends, and then each take up a position suggested by the lie of the land alone, is to me, even if I get no shots, a far more pleasurable way of doing things than being degraded to the level of a shooting machine, posted by a local behind a bush or bank, and told to keep an eye on one particular quarter whence "the Duck are certain to come." And what remarks some of these men do make to encourage you, especially the better dressed and more up-to-date members of the fraternity! I was standing once waiting for Duck on a certain marsh in Sussex, and up sneaked one of these worthies with an insinuating "good evening, sir." Inasmuch as he had a dog with him and I hadn't, I decided to put up with him, though, being a bad shot, I much prefer to miss my birds in solitude.

The sun began to sink below the horizon, and there came echoing over the stillness of the marsh the well-known note of the Ringed Plover. "Ah!" said my mentor, with enthusiasm, "I likes to hear the note of the Curlew; I always thinks it a good sign; it brings the Duck."

I profited to this extent by the remark, that after it I paid more attention to the side from which he didn't expect them than to that from which he did, and my foresight was justified by the event. Not, I would hasten to add, that I regard this individual as in any way typical of the average fowler, at all events on the East Coast. They do know the notes of the birds and the direction from which they may be expected to come, and if I was bent on killing, and nothing else, I should most certainly take one with me if flighting in a new place. My only reason for avoiding them is that, under ordinary circumstances, I would sooner try and do the whole thing myself and fail, than I would have half of it done by another and succeed.

During the evening flight alone does the shore shooter require a dog. In a boat a dog is a terror; on the open shore he is nearly as bad; but when one is flight-shooting he is an invaluable ally. A dog's nose is worth a dozen human eyes when it comes to hunting for a wounded bird in the dark, and, moreover, while he hunts you can shoot.

The most enjoyable evening's flight-shooting that ever came my way was due to an accident. I had taken up my station on a Norfolk marsh behind a gate, expecting one or two shots at the outside. Hardly had I buried myself in the shadow, when up came a bunch of Teal, and I had no sooner settled with them than a flock of Mallard appeared, heading for the same spot. Again I fired, but the survivors, instead of making off for the more distant portion of the marsh, wheeled round, and were soon again within range. This went on for the best part of half an hour, very much to my edification. There seemed some strange attraction about the gate that I had chosen. At last I grasped what they were after: the field next to mine was on a higher level, and, standing on the gate to see if there was anything there to attract them, I discovered that a crop of barley had just been cut, and was not yet gathered in. The mystery was now explained; it was a victory of the stomach over the head.

Barley, too, was accountable for some extraordinary Duck shooting that was once obtained at Holme. A barley ship came ashore near Gore Point, and much of its cargo was scattered upon the beach. Ducks turned up in large numbers, and local sportsmen, clambering on to the wreck, did great execution until the tide returned. But what began amidst much mutual congratulation, was destined to end in the saddest of tragedies; for the shooter who returned first to the wreck after the tide had receded stepped into what he must have imagined to be a shallow pool of water at its side. It was not; it was a deep hole made by the ship when it first struck, but from which it had been shifted by the next tide. The unfortunate man was carried down by his long waders, which, of course, filled, and in this awful death-trap he was drowned before anyone guessed that there was aught amiss.

I myself having always to reckon with a possible attack of rheumatism, have rather a partiality for August and September as flighting months. The advantage in the matter of warmth is obvious, but there is also the matter of variety. During the season of migration one may towards evening meet with many other interesting creatures besides Duck, creatures far more valuable in my eyes than the fattest Mallard or the most delicious Teal. As the light begins to wane, we separate and ensconce ourselves, clad in khaki-coloured habiliments, in some holes in the bank that divides the fresh marshes from the estuary and the shore. Soon a spirit of unrest seems to come over the birds. Such as have hitherto remained unapproachable on the preserved fresh marsh inside the bank, now begin to get on the move. We hear those sprites of darkness, the Common Sandpipers, shrieking along the ditches, and the "peeweet" of the Lapwing echoes incessantly through the gloom.

These we care little about, but perhaps a Dusky Redshank, or, may be, a Wood Sandpiper, is tempted forth to cross the estuary and visit another fresh marsh on the far side, and we make a hurried rush behind the bank to circumvent it, while, if we turn our eyes seawards, party after party of Gulls, numbering as a rule about half a dozen, come stealing up mysteriously out of the grey, and vanish again in a minute in the direction of their nightly stand. We scan each party as it passes on the off-chance of it containing a Little Gull or a Sabine.

"What on earth are those two Wheatears up to?" comes in a stage whisper from the next shelter, where gun Number Two lies concealed; and I look with interest at two birds of this species, which are apparently making darts at something on the ground just in front of us. At first I think they must be catching moths after the manner of Stone Curlews, but soon they reach a streak of moonlight, and I am astonished to see that they are engaged in mobbing a Weasel. The creature, which has probably scented us, takes a series of short runs, after which it halts with uplifted head, and each time it does so the Wheatears make a dart at it and drive it further along. Had this taken place in springtime there would have been no great reason for surprise, since most birds, regardless of size or strength, will attack anything in defence of their young; but we are now in September, and they cannot be nesting. One can only suppose that their actions are attributable to an instinctive hatred of their race's foe.

As the darkness grows more intense, we keep a sharp look out for the Duck, not forgetting, as we are collectors, that this, too, is the time for a rare Owl or a Harrier. The Short-eared Owl turns up frequently on the East Coast in the autumn, and is often flushed by day from the sandhills and the odd heaps of cement and bricks that one meets with here and there along the shore. The Barn Owl I have also encountered; not by day, but during the evening flight. Sometimes, too, one hears the harsh "frank" of the Heron, and it is no uncommon sight to see its long neck dangling from the shoulder of some labourer returning from his visit to the marsh; for many of these men turn out regularly after their day's work is done, and the size of Herons, Curlews, and Whimbrels is sure to draw the fire of an old muzzle-loader. They shoot, of course, mainly for the pot, and there are those who aver that a young Heron makes a savoury dish, though I suspect it requires a good, strong sauce to help it out.

Perhaps the most annoying thing connected with flight-shooting is the difficulty of retrieving the spoils. In winter, you can solace yourself with the reflection that, if you don't manage to retrieve them, the Grey Crows will. It is part of their regular routine work to poke into odd corners and lurking spaces on the chance of unearthing a cripple; but in September these tireless scavengers have not yet arrived, and unless you have a dog with you a bird that is not killed dead will probably baffle your pursuit. I have recently been regaled with two flighting stories, worthy, I think, of being recorded. The first hails from Littlestone, where, in the autumn of 1903, there was a mighty visitation of Teal. They came in one evening in such numbers, flying low over the ground, that a local shooter, after browning them right and left until he ran short of cartridges, was disgusted to find the flight still continuing, while he was impotent to avail himself of it.

Being a man of resource, he at length hit upon a plan; he planted himself firmly on a neighbouring hillock, and, grasping his gun by the barrels, whirled the butt round and round his head like an Indian club until the muscles of his arms gave out, at which point he had succeeded in braining no fewer than five extra birds.

But perhaps the experience of the second sportsman was still more extraordinary. He was riding on a bicycle across Pevensey marshes, preparatory to concealing himself for the flight. Suddenly there was a whirring of wings around him and a smash in front, and amidst discordant "quacks" he found himself in total darkness on the ground. He thought at first that the Ducks, instead of waiting for his assault, had taken time by the forelock and assaulted him; but the more rational explanation that occurred to him, when he had sorted himself, was that the birds had been attracted by his bicycle lamp, and had flown into it much as they might have flown into a lighthouse.

CHAPTER VIII.

PUNTING IN CHICHESTER HARBOUR.

I HAVE never lain with my nose at the tail of a punt gun, and cannot, therefore, dilate on the joys of "putting two and half lbs. of B.B. nicely into a company of several thousand Wigeon." Personally, I have always felt that, granting the undoubted difficulties that lie in the way of such an achievement, there is a suggestion of the "pogrom" about it after all. I would sooner stalk the said thousands with a shoulder gun, and pick out the handsomest drake, than I would train a punt gun on them with such well-timed accuracy as to stretch forty or fifty on the mud. It is the Collector's view, no doubt, not the Sportsman's, and I am quite ready to admit that, if I did set to work to train the punt gun, I should be morally certain to hit the mud, and nothing else.

My experiences of punting, in the sense of shooting from a punt with a shoulder gun, have been confined to Chichester Harbour in the autumn, where, at that season, or, for that matter, at any other season, the question of how to deal with several thousand Wigeon is unlikely to bother anyone, inasmuch as the largest bunch of wild-fowl that I ever encountered there myself consisted of two Teal! There is much to be said, nevertheless, for the harbour as a place wherein to take one's first lessons in punting. To begin with, at Dell Quay you can nearly always secure a punt—there seems no great competition for them—and, what is here no less necessary, a pair of mud-pattens; for the muds are treacherous in the extreme. Secondly, if you can learn to pick your way through the surrounding network of mudflats, when the tide is running out, without getting stuck, you may congratulate yourself on having acquired considerable slimness as a punter; while the man who gains sufficient mastery over the art of what is termed "sculling" to propel his craft against the current that runs past the quay, may henceforth pose almost as a professional; and last, but not least, the place is quiet and unfrequented, so that if you do find yourself stranded on a mudflat, or clinging monkeywise to a mud-embedded oar, while the punt glides away with your feet, there will

be no unseemly cachinnations to distract your attention from the operation in
hand. You may buy your experience dearly, but you will have the fun all to
yourself, and this means something to a sensitive man.

The first time we ever went out we spent a large portion of the morning
in the doleful task of baling out water let in by an ill-fitting cork, and in due
course of time we got stranded while trying to stop the leak. In fact, at Dell
Quay the best thing a beginner can do is to go out just as the tide is coming
in. The muds around are the last covered, and such birds as are about are
sure to visit them. You are thus certain of half an hour's good shooting
without the risk of getting stuck, and, after this, one can put up with the
inconvenience of any stoppage incurred while following the retreating tide.

It must be confessed that after an East Coast estuary, the sport is somewhat tame so far as the prospect of rarities goes. True, I have in my
collection an Avocet killed in Emsworth Creek, and a Black-tailed Godwit
said to have come from Siddlesham, but, as a rule, it is the sort of place where
one looks upon a Redshank or Little Stint as a good bird, though the part
near Appledram Sluice is noted for Green Sandpipers, one of which birds once
nearly cost me a ducking, for I risked a standing shot to get it, and the punt,
which had been guaranteed by its owner as a conveyance wherein one might
circumnavigate the Isle of Wight in safety, was sorely tried so far as balance
went, when I staggered round it after the recoil. Common Sandpipers also
frequent the drains opposite the sluice, while there is a projecting corner just
beyond, from which one can get shots at most of the smaller waders as they
fly round on their way to the last muds of all.

The reed-fringed water near Fishbourne is doubtless the place where,
according to Captain Knox, a famous gunner named Carter once secured two
Bearded Tits; and the drains and small streams in these meadows nearly
always have in the autumn a good sprinkling of Kingfishers. They often
stray into the estuary itself, and may be seen sitting on any small posts along
its margin.

The Turtle Dove is another bird here commonly met with. They are
very numerous on the inland fields, and often come down to the edge of the
saltings, like the domestic pigeons from the Fishbourne farms. At times I
have seen a Cormorant flying heavily near the old mill, and the commoner
Gulls, with an occasional Greater Black-back, scatter over the mudflats as
soon as ever the tide goes down. Wading deep at the edge of the tideway, or
sitting hunched up in sombre exclusiveness, will be found as a rule at least
one Heron, often more; but the Herons here are well able to take care of
themselves, and are a very different race to their New Forest relatives on the

Beaulieu River. They are perhaps the most interesting birds in the harbour, and with good glasses one can watch their fishing operations without difficulty, even from the top of the sea wall.

As the tide went down, we used to drift past the Quay, and make our way towards Itchenor, and anyone wanting a Curlew or Whimbrel was likely to find some feeding on these extensive muds. Bringing a Curlew to bag is a very different matter to finding it, as all shore shooters are well aware;

THE JOYS OF PUNTING.

indeed, in such open localities whistling and lying up in their line of flight, if there happens to be any cover, are the only methods that ever meet with much success.

In Norfolk, on the other hand, I have thrice almost trodden on the bird. Where there are bushes at the edge of the saltings, they are wont to harbour in these, when the wind is in certain quarters, and having once got into them they trust to the cover they afford and lie as well as game birds. There is something almost ludicrous in the way a Curlew makes off if you do happen to surprise him; the situation must seem so strange to a bird which generally decamps outside a hundred yards. Snipe and game birds are accustomed to rising under people's feet, but a Curlew evidently is not ; he seems for the moment utterly " flabbergasted," and as he sheers off with a helpless "whaup" he presents the easiest of shots. Whimbrels, or as the locals here call them, " Titterels," are also common on these flats, and though they will not readily let themselves be approached, even in a punt, yet they are the easiest of all large shore birds to whistle up; a novice can imitate the note quite well enough to bring a new arrival into range, and they then afford a very simple shot.

I have heard the mouth of the harbour spoken of as a good place for Wild Geese, and as I know that they are often hawked about Emsworth in hard weather, it is probable that my informant spoke the truth. I remember also reading in the paper that two Black-tailed Godwits had been shot near Portsmouth, and from the same neighbourhood came the report of the shooting of five Cranes !

However, the enthusiasm of the shooter who perpetrated this massacre must have received a well-earned damper the following week, when a caustic letter in the local paper suggested that he might be interested to hear that on the day in question five of these birds had escaped from Sanger's Circus, which was then performing in the town !

CHAPTER IX.

THE DOWNS.

THE wanderer over the Southern Downs may expect to meet with fine air, fine scenery, and, under normal circumstances, one fine bird—the Stone Curlew. Salisbury Plain, indeed, could boast once of a yet nobler denizen in the Great Bustard. It was one of the last refuges of that splendid bird, and it was here that sportsmen are said to have coursed it with greyhounds. Now the combined efforts of the husbandman, the golfer, and the War Office have banished it from its haunts for ever; and lucky indeed will be the visitor who gets a distant glimpse of a Peregrine, or even a Merlin, during a sojourn lasting for a week. Peregrines do frequent it at times all the same, and the story of the Salisbury Canon, who stocked his larder by robbing the eyrie of some Peregrines on the Cathedral roof, has this much truth in it—that the birds have been known to haunt it for some considerable periods, and have even dropped eggs in the spouting.

Merlins turn up pretty often in the autumn, and, when Falconers go there after Larks at that season, wild birds have been known to join the trained ones in their pursuit; but, when all is said and done, I feel bound to record the damaging testimony of an enthusiast who has often visited the locality, and states that he has never seen anything more exciting than a Golden Plover. Personally, though I have roamed the Downs at various seasons for over twenty years, the Kestrel and Sparrowhawk are the only raptorial birds that I have ever seen on them, and even the Sparrowhawk has of late become quite rare. Nevertheless, as recently as 1901, I stumbled on three playing together on the ground in company with three Magpies, and enjoyed for the nonce the unique experience of putting up a veritable covey of predatory birds!

Towards the end of the last century I remember admiring a splendid specimen of the Kite which had just been killed near Alresford, and had found its way to Chalkley's shop at Winchester, and in conversation with a gamekeeper near the same city, I was told how he had watched a huge "Buzzard Hawk" fly across his warren in the preceding spring, the bird just keeping clear of his ambush, and passing on its way unscathed. I was more interested myself in his account of some Hobbies which had nested the year before in the hillside coverts, and paid the usual penalty for their temerity. I put in a word on their behalf, and extracted the confession that "they did seem simple-minded little creatures, certainly."

Simple-mindedness, however, is probably the most unfortunate quality that a Hawk can possess, and though he offered to let any such future visitors alone until I arrived to deal with them, I saw that the concession partook only of the nature of a reprieve, and that after I had secured my pair the death sentence would soon be executed on the remaining birds. As a matter of fact, when I visited the wood in the following August, no trace of Hobbies was to be found.

Kestrels may still be called common on the Downs. I watched seven one day all in the air at once, calling to one another as they sailed backwards and forwards over the rolling plain. Whether they escaped I know not, for they were absurdly tame, and I could have shot four that morning had I desired to do so.

As for Harriers, on the Downs proper I have never seen or heard of one, but the fir copses are the regular resort of numerous Long-eared Owls, which may be found at times drawn bolt upright against the trunks, sometimes under the shelter of an old nest. They seem more inclined to move by day than the other species. These same copses are also regularly frequented by Carrion Crows, Jays, and Magpies, the latter seeming, however, to prefer the small clumps of beeches with which many of the hills are crowned. In these they build their nests, and may often be seen feeding in the long grass around them. The difference between the behaviour of the Magpie here and in the Channel Islands is most marked. In Guernsey they were numerous and impudent, but there was no game, and no one shot them, the result being that they used even to frequent the gardens in the town. In Hampshire, the most one sees of them is a flicker of black and white as they shuffle off from the beeches the moment one emerges from the nearest copse.

And now to come to the one fine bird that we may fairly hope to meet with on the Downs—the bird *par excellence* of the district—the Stone Curlew. This interesting link between the lost Bustard and the Plovers is probably far commoner in Hampshire than is generally supposed. On Farley Mount my brother has seen a flock of twenty-three in the autumn. I have heard of equally large numbers elsewhere. Nor is this all; it is generally distributed, and pairs may be met with on many of the higher

E. C. ARNOLD PINXT.]

THE ANXIOUS PARENT. (*Stone Curlews.*)

[WEST NEWMAN.

ranges during the breeding season, though its habit of either decamping early, or lying prone with neck outstretched, causes it to be overlooked unless its presence is previously suspected. In the evening it is more easily discovered. It is then far more active than by day, and places, which in the morning appeared untenanted, will now re-echo with its cry. I have found the eggs once after a two and a half hours' search on a typical stone-covered hill. I saw the bird get up and run as I began to ascend the slope, and then lost sight of her, and when a Lapwing rose shortly afterwards I thought it must have been the runner. A Stone-Curlew then rose on the other side, and I wasted much time hunting in that direction, and it was only just at the last, when about to abandon the search, that I went to the spot where I saw the original runner, and almost immediately lighted on the eggs; the bird had run in a semicircle before taking wing. The eggs were easier to see than I had anticipated; they caught my eye when I was quite ten yards off, though there was no nest, and though they were amongst stones of very similar colour.

But for its squatting propensity, the Stone-Curlew would be a most difficult bird to bring to bag, and it was long ere I obtained a specimen. In despair I descended once to the setting of traps among the gorse bushes I caught one hedgehog, and injured several sheep, and then, returning to more orthodox methods, I became at length, after an ever-memorable chase, the proud possessor of a Hampshire bird. Carefully ascending the hill where I had once found the eggs, I soon saw the well-known form silhouetted against the sky-line, and looking uncommonly as if about to fly. I resorted to the oft-tried circle dodge, and sheered off to the right, and the bird, also changing its intention, proceeded to run instead. At this moment an unexpected obstacle presented itself in the shape of a second bird on the other side of me, and looking equally inclined to fly. Somewhat disconcerted by this *embarras de richesse*, for to have put up either bird would have been fatal, I sneaked along half-way between the two with my head down, and eyes half-closed, and thirty yards further on I saw that I should get a shot at the right-hand bird, which had also taken to running, and was now crouching behind some wire. Suddenly up it got, and rather flustered me by taking several beats straight towards where I stood. As it sheered sharply off I let drive with both barrels, and, to my unspeakable disgust, away it went apparently unharmed, while the second bird rose with a whirr behind me, and was soon also out of range. After weeks of stalking and scheming, I had lost the prize when almost within my very grasp. But no; as I turned for a farewell look at my

E

intended victim preparatory to entering on what I knew would be a boot-less pursuit of the second bird, I suddenly thought I noticed the shimmering flight that so often heralds a collapse, and, sure enough, a moment afterwards up went its wings, and the bird fell headlong to the ground. I rushed up and found it lying stone dead within a few yards of a thick coppice; had it gone a little further I should probably have lost it even then. I owed my success entirely to the Stone-Curlew's readiness to crouch, and, as most persons find it so hard to get within range, I cannot help thinking that the formation of the ground at this particular place makes the birds unusually ready to adopt these tactics. Half a mile off we are visible to them, and then disappear into a gully. If they don't go then, we are within two hundred yards at our next appearance, and possibly catch them in two minds, a state of things that results in their adopting the more timid policy of crouching. If the slope were gradual, I believe that they would always take wing at about three hundred yards.

One can hardly leave the Stone-Curlew without reference to the exhaustive account of the actions of an East Anglian colony contributed to the pages of the 'Zoologist' by Mr. Selous. The writer was enabled to get quite close to a large flock day after day for two months, and during that period he acquired a most interesting insight into the habits of these extraordinary birds. His description of their evening chase after moths and other insects, some of them on the wing, is paralleled in my own experience by the behaviour of a tame Lesser Black-backed Gull, which never seemed so happy as when a swarm of insects descended on the lawn. His antics must have been very similar to those of the Stone-Curlews, for he caught his prey both settled and flying, sometimes using his wings to aid him, and sometimes merely darting along the ground.

Another interesting member of the Plover tribe, which is supposed to visit the downs for a few days on migration, is the Dotterel. I have never had the good fortune to meet with it myself except in Norfolk, by the sea-shore, and I fancy that its route lies through Kent and Sussex rather than Hampshire.

The beautiful Lapwing, whose aerial gambols lend such a charm to springtime, is, I am glad to say, rapidly recovering its numbers. At one time, round Winchester it seemed to have reached the verge of extinction as a breeding species, and many were the uplands on which it had ceased to rear its young. Now, thanks to some unknown cause, perhaps the fact that it did not pay to spend an afternoon hunting for its eggs, its wild note and strange drumming can again be heard in most of its old haunts, and the birds seem thoroughly to have re-established themselves.

Of the smaller species to be met with, I should put the Nightjar first. The bird breeds upon the bleak hillsides, which are also, early in August, the favourite haunt of the Silver-spotted Skipper, and is especially to be looked for where a few small thorn bushes stand out upon the downs amidst the remnants of defunct furze-brakes. These patches are generally bare, and have sundry old flints upon them, and the dead sticks of furze themselves closely harmonize with the plumage of the sitting bird. I have also put them up during the daytime from the middle of the road, and more often from the bracken in the copses.

The ponds which exist here and there upon the downs are the regular rendezvous of many small birds for purposes of ablution, and it is the custom of juvenile fowlers to set limed straws around them in the autumn. Wonderful, indeed, is the variety of a successful afternoon's bag. Wheatears, Pipits, Goldfinches, Linnets, Greenfinches, Buntings, and Wagtails all get entangled in the deadly snare, and after vigorous but unavailing struggles are thrust into the dark box through the leg of an old stocking, which offers the only means of entrance and exit from the gloomy depths of this receptacle. Sometimes the birds are caught outright; at others they take flight with the fatal straw attached to tail or pinion, and after a few beats the lime adheres to some other part of the body, and the victim falls helpless to the ground. Immediately there is a rush of a ragged figure from the far side of the pond, the captive is seized, released none too gently, and hurried without ceremony into the box.

Many of the boys, often golf caddies, who engage in this method of bird-catching, exhibit considerable knowledge of the habits and notes of the birds, and one cannot help sympathising with their excitement when some valuable stranger is threading his dangerous path amongst the snares. Wheatears and Buntings are the most difficult to secure; Greenfinches rush blindly to their doom.

From one of these ponds I once flushed a Redshank in springtime, and once in the autumn a flock of shore birds, probably Grey Plover, passed high over my head.

At times during the August migration we are visited by some Tree Pipits. I was once enabled to follow a flock of twenty for some miles along a hillside. My attention was attracted by their soft single note, not unlike that of a Spotted Flycatcher, and, on a closer inspection, I saw that they were longer and more tawny than our local Titlark. The light margins of the wing-coverts and tertiaries showed up clearly as they ran along the ground, while the rump appeared uniform at quite a

E 2

short distance. Their movements were much like those of Wagtails. They often darted up for a moment to secure an insect, and I saw one miss a butterfly, though settled on a flower. They were accompanied by a sprinkling of Whinchats, a bird which, like the Stonechat, is generally distributed in suitable places throughout the district.

In winter the bleak expanse of downland has few attractions for the naturalist. A small flock of Goldfinches is about the most one can hope to meet with, and it is satisfactory to be able to record that, like the Lapwing, the Goldfinch appears to be steadily recovering its numbers. If there are any about, they will be on those portions of the downs which are dotted at intervals with thistles, and their merry note and glancing wings will soon draw attention to their presence. Such other birds as are to be found will mostly frequent the neighbourhood of ricks, and here in hard weather Bramblings and Cirl-Buntings may sometimes be secured, the latter being easy to overlook, and more rarely we get a flying visit from the Snow-Bunting; but as a rule the smaller birds seem at this season to find their way into the less exposed meadows near the river, and there is little to interest one on the downs.

Though the furze and heather-clad heaths which are to be found near Aldershot and in Dorsetshire can hardly be termed downs, yet a mention of the birds to be found there may perhaps most fittingly be inserted in the present chapter. Stonechats and Titlarks are of course common upon them, but there are two more interesting species which seem specially partial to their wild expanse. The first of these is Montagu's Harrier. Perhaps to-day the commonest of the British Harriers, it still makes an occasional effort to rear a brood in these localities, and though there is no great probability of a stranger meeting with one on any given day, a person who has an eye to likely places may with luck tumble on the bird. There is no mistaking it if you do, the long peaked wings and light grey plumage at once attracting attention as it flies across the sombre plain. A splendid old male, which I put up in April, 1900, from beside a brackish pool in the midst of a Dorset heath, showed no marked symptoms of alarm at my presence, but settled contentedly about eighty yards off on a furze bush, and allowed me to have a steady look at him before he at length took wing.

I have several times since visited the heath in question in the hope of meeting another, but I have never again seen a sign of one, and I now regard the above-mentioned bird as having been a sort of avine Last of the Mohicans, which very possibly never found a mate. Indeed, the heath

E. C. ARNOLD PINXT.]　　AN AVINE "LAST OF THE MOHICANS."　(*Montagu's Harrier.*)　[WEST NEWMAN.

itself is much smaller than I originally supposed, though it might no doubt support a bachelor Harrier on short commons, if the keepers would leave him to himself.

The other species referred to is one dear to all British ornithologists—the Dartford Warbler, that fascinating little oddity—part Wren, part Tit, part Warbler, which braves, but alas! not always successfully, the utmost rigour of our English cold. What a difficult bird it is to discover! What a difficult bird to secure when found! No wonder that all collectors are so eager to possess a specimen of this odd-voiced, odd-shaped denizen of our southern heaths. Ere I found it at last in Dorsetshire, I had traversed miles of furze-brakes on the Hampshire and Sussex downs, but, convinced at length that its true home was on the sandy soil, where furze and heather combine, I took the train into the above-mentioned county, examined the scenery as I went along, got out when it seemed most like my ideal Dartford country, and cast around for a likely spot. Half a mile along the road I struck a promising piece of heath, entered it, and put up two Dartfords within two minutes of my arrival. Then began the fun. Not having seriously expected to find the birds, I had only the smallest sized walking-stick gun with me, and that in such foul condition that its shooting powers were almost nil. However, with this weapon I started in pursuit, and the Dartfords responding gallantly, I chivvied them about for the space of one hour, during which I actually got in one ineffectual shot. They never kept still for a moment, but flitted continuously from bush to bush, and one could never quite spot them in the furze until just as they took wing for the next patch.

At length the sun went in, a cold wind sprang up, the Dartfords got into a large patch of furze, and there they remained triumphant, masters of the situation for that day, at all events. As far as I could see, there were four on the heath. I can't say they struck me as being much like Long-tailed Wrens. Their flight, to my mind, was more like that of a Long-tailed Tit, at all events at the start; it developed into the dart of a Warbler as they neared the next bush. It was, in fact, very difficult to keep them in view against the dark background of the furze, and when they got the wind behind them they were often blown along like shuttlecocks. So long as the sun was out they showed no inclination to skulk, but when they did begin their persistency was disconcerting in the extreme; there was absolutely no getting them out, and I can quite believe that one might overlook half a dozen on a dull day.

Armed with a better weapon, I went again on the following morning. The sun was shining brightly, and the birds were now at the top of the furze bushes pouring out their extraordinary song. During this performance, with their tails standing almost bolt upright, their throat feathers expanded and crests erect, they were most comic objects to behold—they seemed all head and tail. For some time I failed to get one even now; they always dropped down just when you didn't expect it, and I was also hampered by several untimely interruptions. About noon the sun, as on the preceding day, went in; in went the Dartfords too, and, with the sky rapidly clouding over, I began to think I was doomed to a second failure. Though I tramped through the furze and heaved stones till my arm was tired, I could get nothing out, and at last in despair I took a stroll to a distant part of the heath. Here, while resting, I suddenly heard a soft, low note 'at the bottom of the furze. As it was followed by a harsher one, I went down on hands and knees and crawled in towards the sound. A second note directed me to the exact spot, and there I descried a Dartford pottering about a couple of feet above the ground. Once again I was struck by the similarity of its actions to those of a Long-tailed Tit, but I had little time for observation; the chance was too good to be frittered away, and a lucky shot between the furze stems secured at length the bird that I had sought so long in vain.

Three years later I again visited the heath to see how the Dartfords were getting on, and was delighted to find them quite as numerous as before. I noted again that when singing they seem all head and tail, which they then tilt to its highest point, while when they fly they seem all hind quarters with no head. During their song the feathers are puffed out, but at times they are very compact, and have a peculiarly sheeny appearance in the sun. They seemed partial to furze that was of mature age, with open spaces below. I never saw them where it was short and green. On this occasion I had the luck to watch a pair building their nest. It was in a small furze-bush, and was very neat and strong for a Warbler's, being made of broad, whitish moorland grass. The birds repeatedly flew, one might almost say dived, from some tall furze on the top of a stone wall into the main furze-brake beneath, returning each time with some whitish object in their beaks. I thought at first that these were moths, and that they must have young, though it was only April 25th. However, I eventually found the nest; there was nothing in it, and the supposed moths turned out to be small pieces of the whitest portion of furze blossoms, which the birds were using to line the nest. I saw one bird rise once, and warble for a few seconds in the air like a Pipit.

CHAPTER X.

THE BUSHES.

Of recent years perhaps no haunt of the collector has attracted to itself so much attention as the strip of shingle which runs along the Norfolk coast between Wells and Cromer. A large portion of this strip is interspersed with a thick dwarf scrub (*Sueda fruticosa*), rarely rising beyond three feet in height, especially at the beginning of August. The walking is atrocious, and the collector who visits the locality for the first time is almost sure to instinctively avoid what he will afterwards come to regard as the most interesting portion of his beat.

But the day, or rather evening, soon arrives when, seated beside the operating table of the local taxidermist, he listens, for a time, indeed, with the ear of the sceptic, to the tales of surpassing rarities shot or observed upon this very beach. He hears how Messrs Gurney and Power discovered that these bushes, for years immune and unfrequented by the gunner, are the regular resort of a vast army of migratory small birds, and that, given only a favourable wind, there is no reason why the choicest of the Warblers may not be brought home in triumph by the veriest novice that ever handled a gun. Well do I remember listening with incredulity to the story of the Yellow-browed Warbler at which some workman let fly his muzzle-loader merely to get rid of the charge; and of the Aquatic which flew thrice round a collector, while his companion vainly exhorted him to fire at what he believed to be a Sedge-Warbler, and not worth the expenditure of a cartridge. The glories of Dr. Power's Barred and Icterine Warblers were also expatiated on for our edification, and, fired at length by the recital of these successes, and more especially by the appearance in the flesh of an Icterine shot by Mr. Robert Gurney, we determined on the next day to give the bushes a genuine trial.

Now the bushes are a lottery and the prizes few; but there is a fascination about "doing" them, which appeals to young and old alike. One can always guarantee two hours' solid exercise for the thighs, and an impromptu bath into the bargain if it happens to have rained during the night, but beyond this nothing is certain. You may tramp them from end to end and see nothing, and another shooter coming half an hour later may find himself surrounded with migrants in fresh from the sea. I have heard, though I have never seen it, of the bushes being " smothered " with birds. Or again, the birds may be in the bushes and refuse to come out, in which case, as far as you are concerned, they might just as well not be there at all. Various methods have been tried to effect their ejection. Some have hired men to beat with sticks, others have dragged ropes across the top, and ordinary individuals simply take the bull by the horns and tramp through them; but, generally speaking, the birds either come out rapidly of their own accord, or skulk and remain unmoved by any device.

When they do pop out, they are still many degrees removed from the cabinet. In the first place, you may fire too soon and blow them to pieces, or, while refraining until they have reached the requisite distance, wait too long, and see them unexpectedly vanish in the scrub; and sometimes, most maddening of all, when the bird is brought to bag uninjured, subsequent exposure or shaking causes it to go bad before the day is out. Most people prefer a twelve-bore loaded with a half-charge of No. 8, while others advocate dust-shot packed very loosely. But, whatever charge be used, I am convinced that if a real rarity is obtained it should be carried in the hand, head downwards, to allow the juices to escape, with a thin piece of paper wrapped loosely round the body, and, even before this is done, the bird should be laid on the sand beneath the shade of a bush until it has had time to stiffen.

My own experiences of the bushes have been varied and typical in the main. Entering them for the first time one bright September morning, we were greeted at once by the well-known note of the Titlark, and later on some Whinchats and dubious-looking Reed-Buntings perched temptingly on the higher sprays.

Suddenly there is the flicker of a red tail between some twigs, and out darts the owner like a flash. At first sight it appears to be a Redstart, but ere its species can be surely decided, it is buried again in the thickest recesses of the cover. A few vigorous kicks put it out once more into the open, and a second glance reveals the welcome fact that the red only covers half the tail, and thus proclaims the presence of that delightful Arctic visitor, the Bluethroat. It falls to my brother's gun, and proves to be a perfect specimen of an immature bird, disappointing only in the absence of the blue gorget, which is at this age replaced by a ring of

French-grey spots. Having duly wrapped it in paper and ensconced it behind a bush, we returned with fresh ardour to the scrub; but, though two perspiring bipeds worked the remaining portions for several hours with all the zeal begotten of success, they saw nothing else worth shooting at, except a pair of Pied Flycatchers which appeared towards evening on some tall horned-poppies near the beach. Two days later I bagged an adult Bluethroat within fifty yards of the same spot, and in the afternoon we thought at one time that we had stumbled on an Aquatic Warbler. However, such portions of it as survived a combined bombardment on the

DOING THE BUSHES.

part of two excited guns turned out to be the relics of a Sedge-Warbler, and another disappointment followed when I shot a Wryneck under the impression that it was a Barred Warbler. A Wryneck seems at first sight an unlikely bird to encounter in such a place, but even Green Woodpeckers have sometimes been got there, and we ourselves saw one, not far off, the following year.

The Bluethroat is the bird in search of which most collectors first visit the bushes, but they do not all secure one. Some years none are seen, and, moreover, the date of their arrival varies much. It requires also a quick eye to distinguish them on the wing, the orange on the tail showing less than one might suppose from looking at the stuffed bird.

In size and shape they resemble Robins more than Redstarts, and they have a darker look than the Redstart as they fly. Few would imagine from seeing an old bird on the wing how beautiful they are in the hand. Most of those shot have only a blue gorget, and the shade of blue varies, sometimes having a mauve tint in it, and at others being brighter and more metallic. I once shot one with blue moustaches as well as a splendid breast, and another that came under my notice had a blue throat into the bargain.

The capture of a rarity is almost always followed by a general, if somewhat illogical, invasion of the bushes on the succeeding day. All the local gunners turn out for the occasion, and ill indeed does it fare with any unfortunate Warblers that may happen to be harbouring there at the time. Numerous Redstarts fall victims to those who are in pursuit of the Bluethroat, and many Willow-Wrens pay the penalty of greatness in being so closely allied to the much prized Icterine.

But perhaps the bird that it is most easy to mistake for a good one is, curiously enough, the Robin! It seems absurd at first sight, but the fact is a Robin in the bushes on migration is a very different creature to the familiar inhabitant of our gardens, and at times it is most difficult to identify it. You don't see the red on the breast at all, and what you think you see is a strange dark Warbler with a flight that may mean anything. I never feel in the least surprised when anyone tells me that he has shot a Robin by mistake.

I remember, the day after the killing of an Aquatic, meeting two fisher boys returning from a raid. One of them carried a sack, and from the depths of this receptacle they retrieved at length two birds which they asked me to identify. They proved to be a Whinchat and a Titlark, but sometimes it is the other way altogether. A shooter came into the local naturalist's one evening with half a dozen shore birds to have them examined. The best was a Knot, and he was retiring with evident disappointment.

"Sure you have nothing else, sir?" said the Professor, whose experience of beginners was a lengthy one.

"Well, only some sort of a Shrike in my pocket," replied the sportsman, and out he fished, to the general amazement, a Barred Warbler! The supposition, however, was not so wide of the mark as one might suppose, for Dr. Power told me that when he shot his, it did sit up and behave itself very much after the manner of a Shrike. Still, the bird here referred to was shot while skulking during a short squall, which very probably brought it down to its doom.

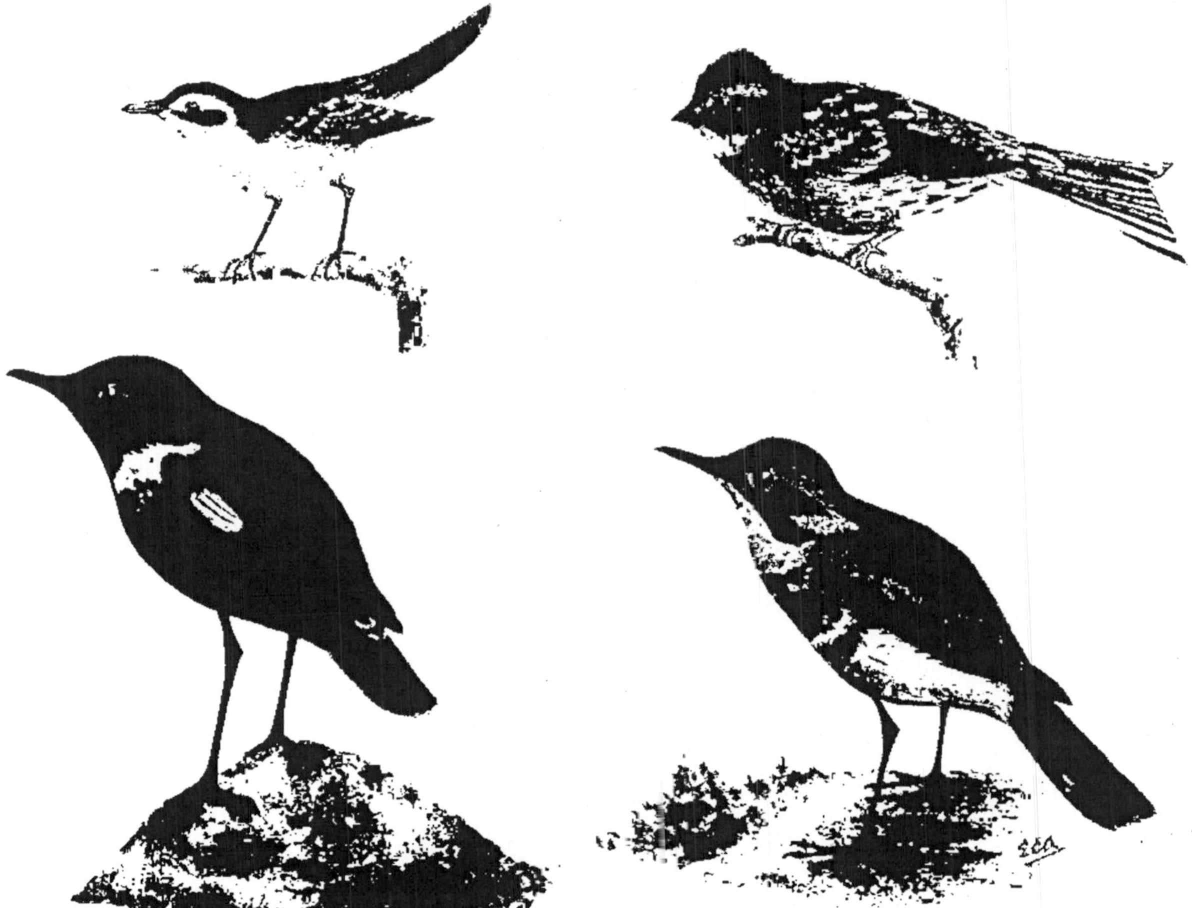

E. C. ARNOLD PINXT.] [WEST NEWMAN.

A word on the subject of indiscriminate slaughter. Quite apart from
the cruelty, very little comes of it. A shooter who takes the trouble to
notice the common birds carefully will, in nine cases out of ten (the tenth
being the Robin), spot the rarity as different if he comes upon it. It was
so at all events in the case of the Icterine which I had the good luck to
secure on September 5th, 1899. At the end of a long and unsuccessful
day's shooting in the estuary, I turned aside from the homeward track
towards the bushes, already worked through in the morning, as a last
chance of picking up something rare. They had just been thrashed out by
another collector, and I myself had seen nothing in them before; but no
matter, I knew that went for little. I would just try one favourite beat,
"the first sandhill bushes," a bare one hundred yards of the tallest scrub.
Before I had traversed ten of them, out popped a Warbler, and, little as
the Icterine differs from the Willow Wren, I guessed at once what it was.
The shape was different, and though the back view and wings with their
light-coloured tertiaries were suggestive in a way of an immature Pied
Flycatcher, I had caught a glimpse of the yellow breast, and eagerly
hastened in pursuit. From over-excitement I missed more than once, but
at length getting in a clear shot as it darted for a moment across the
sand, I rushed up, and shortly afterwards experienced the most delightful
of all sensations as I gazed on the large tell-tale beak of a genuine
Hypolais icterina.

Kind indeed has fortune been to me since that eventful day. On
September 13th, 1904, I was shooting the bushes with my brother, G. F. The
whole place swarmed with Linnets, and, remembering that it was out of a flock
of Linnets that Dr. Power got his Ortolan, I remarked jokingly to a rival
shooter, as I passed him, that I was going out to get an Ortolan. A
quarter of a mile on, up got a lightish bird, which I momentarily took to
be a Lark. By the time it was out of range its flight and more mellow
note had told me that it was something else, and I rushed round the sand-
hills to get another look at it. Here my brother joined me, and we put the
bird up and missed it. It was now quite clear that it was a stranger, and,
though it rose wild the next time, I just got in a shot, and secured thereby
fame as a prophet—and, what pleased me more, an Ortolan! It lacked the
beautiful plumage of the adult male, but had nevertheless a fine flush of
chestnut on the flanks. It was a bird that one might easily have passed
over owing to its insignificant appearance on the wing; its flight was swift
and low, not heavy like that of the Corn-Bunting or Yellowhammer; it
reminded me rather of the flight of a Garden-Warbler.

On the 2nd of the same month my brother, G. F., had secured a far greater rarity in the shape of a Siberian Stonechat (*Pratincola maura*) — the first specimen ever taken in the British Isles. This bird he shot on a gorse common not far off, and he all but threw it away. He was induced to shoot by the bird's unusually dark appearance, but on picking it up he found that it was moulting heavily and that the dark look was in a great measure due to this. He fortunately brought it home, and I had it stuffed on the off-chance of its turning out a melanism. For over a year it remained in my collection, a seedy-looking bird, which I regarded with no particular respect, and then Mr. Howard Saunders saw and identified it, and it was subsequently exhibited at the British Ornithologists' Club. It returned from that ordeal invested with the halo of renown, and I now shudder to think how near we came to making away with it. It is in the Eastbourne Museum.

The following year I had the extraordinary good luck to add another bird to the British list—*viz.*, the Yellow-breasted Bunting (*Emberiza aureola*), and, had I followed the advice of several people who saw it in the flesh, it too might have been thrown away. This was a genuine case of patience being rewarded. The season of 1905 was in the early part of September an unusually bad one. Day after day people went through the bushes and hardly a shot was fired. Some left the village, some ceased to do the bushes, and in the end I, as the only person who stuck to them, had the shooting almost to myself. Up till the 14th the wind was mostly S.W.; it then veered to N.W., and on the 19th I got a Landrail out of the scrub. On the 20th, with the wind still N.W., Mr. A. H. Streeten and I unquestionably saw, and missed, a Red-breasted Flycatcher. The bird flew straight at me, and settled a few yards off. I had a good view, and noted that it was smaller than a Pied Flycatcher, and had white in the tail, but none on the wings. For fear of blowing it to bits I retired too far and managed to miss it, and, as it unfortunately flew out over the muds, we never again got on its track. However, the meeting with this bird proved a stepping-stone towards the acquisition of the Bunting. Having decided that if the Flycatcher had returned from its excursion into the estuary, it had probably got into the "Watch House" bushes, we did these with elaborate care the following day, and though no Flycatcher was to be found, we suddenly put out a bird, which from its flight and size appeared to be a very yellow specimen of a Titlark. Still there was a doubt about it, and so we started on a chase, which proved eminently discreditable to our shooting powers. After each miss I became more convinced that the bird was a rarity; but, when it was at length laid low, we both thought at first that it was a young Yellowhammer, buoyant though the flight had been; its streaked rump then attracted my attention, and also the arrangement of the white on the tail feathers, and, taking these peculiarities in conjunction with the fact that it had a very distinct broad yellow eye-stripe, I finally decided to stuff it. I then took it to the British Museum, where it was identified by Dr. Bowdler Sharpe, and afterwards by Mr. Howard Saunders, who exhibited it with the Stonechat at the British Ornithologists' Club. The bird is now in the Eastbourne Museum.

As regards the killing of these rare migrants, I consider it justifiable. They are abnormal wanderers, which would never settle in England, and it seems far better that they should be carefully preserved for the benefit of those who would otherwise never see them, rather than be observed through glasses by one individual for the space of perhaps half an hour at the outside.

On the whole, the first three weeks in September seem the best time for the bushes, but the learned disagree concerning the most favourable wind. The majority, I believe, vote for a nor-wester with drizzling rain; but it appears more probable that the arrival or non-arrival of the birds depends upon the direction of the wind at the point whence they start, rather than on what is blowing along the Norfolk coast.

The following list of birds obtained in the bushes may, though doubtless incomplete, prove interesting and perhaps encouraging to those who have often, like the writer, tramped through them from start to finish without indulging in a single shot.

LIST OF BIRDS.

Barred Warbler.	Pallas's Willow-Warbler.
Icterine Warbler.	Aquatic Warbler.
Bluethroat.	Yellow-browed Warbler.
Ortolan. .	Ring-Ouzel.
Shore-Lark.	Wryneck.
Nightjar.	Green Woodpecker.
Pied Flycatcher.	Richard's Pipit.
Lapland Bunting.	Red-breasted Flycatcher.
Great Grey Shrike.	Yellow-breasted Bunting.
Landrail.	

CHAPTER XI.

BY BRACKISH POOL AND ODOROUS STREAM.

THERE are few portions of our low-lying coasts which have not behind them a fringe of semi-drained marsh land, used chiefly for pasturing cattle, and subject in wild weather to occasional inroads of the sea. It follows that there will be left behind a sprinkling of brackish pools, sometimes even so numerous as to form a regular marsh, as in the case of Thorpe Mere at Aldeburgh. While in other places may be seen small streams of fresh but odorous water trickling with tortuous course towards the sea.

These marshes are nowadays, for the most part, preserved, and, though they harbour little game, the disputes and bad feeling which have almost always accompanied their enclosure generally make it a difficult matter for any stranger to get leave to shoot there. The method of enclosing them is at all events a simple one. Some local magnate having duly expatiated on the advantages sure to result to the community from land-reclaiming, proceeds first to the erection of a sea-wall. The wall erected, he erects also notice-boards to warn off trespassers, and if any old gunners, accustomed from boyhood to shoot over the marshes, object and seem likely to cause trouble, they are *given leave* to shoot over them. New-comers are ejected, though at times a stranger is turned off and afterwards given leave, in order to establish the principle of leave-getting. Soon the rising generation begins to look on the land as private, and thus all free shooting becomes a thing of the past.

One cannot help suggesting that any shore shooter, able to stand the expense of a prosecution for trespass, might do much service to local gunners, and himself get good sport in a double sense out of a persistent disregard of these notice-boards. In many cases, if the accosted shooter presented his card with a statement that he believed the shooting to be public, and intended to shoot there until actually prosecuted, it is doubtful whether any further steps would be taken, and still more doubtful whether anything would come of them if they were.

However, to return to the winged denizens of these unsavoury wastes.

We will follow first a certain Sussex streamlet, which, permeated by the refuse of a tan-yard through which it passes, flows after many windings into a well-known estuary of the sea. It is an ideal haunt of Sandpipers. The banks, smothered with vegetation and dotted with tall bushes and an occasional willow, slope sharply down on either side, at times overhanging the red-brown stream beneath. The water is crossed at intervals by convenient resting places in the shape of wooden rails, and at low tide miniature mudflats are exposed to view, the stench being then unbearable—*i.e.*, to human nostrils, for Sandpipers seem to revel in it. It is clear that snap shots will

SETTLING DOWN FOR THE DUCK.

be the order of the day, and as we reach the second corner there is a sharp shriek, the flash of a white rump between the branches of a willow, and almost before the gun can reach the shoulder a Green Sandpiper has mounted to the skies. We know that it is a "Green" and not a "Common" Sandpiper by the momentary vision of the white rump—that conspicuous ornament which distinguishes afar many a rare bird from some similar but commoner species. A white rump may indeed be regarded as the hall-mark of avine gentility. To the novice, who scans the flocks of Chaffinches amongst the snow-covered fields, it is this that betrays the long-sought Brambling. By its aid we can tell at a glance that a Sandpiper is not a Common one, and on the shore it is always welcome among the smaller

Waders if only because' it is 'a certain proof that we are not pursuing the "inevitable" Dunlin.

So much for the attractions of the white rump. We were destined to see other Green Sandpipers before we left the drain. As we stood gazing at 'the departed bird, his cries were answered by a like note from behind, and we glanced round in time to discover that a second bird had lain *perdu* at the preceding bend, and had now risen to rejoin' its mate. To make matters worse, a shot, fired hurriedly and without effect, put up a small family party which was breakfasting one hundred yards ahead, and we had the additional satisfaction of seeing the whole flock assemble, and after circling round once or twice, far out of range, make straight off for the harbour, or some still more distant retreat. We now planned a drive on the chance of the drain holding some more birds. Making a detour of more than half a mile, I posted myself beside the entrance of the sluice into the estuary, and waited while my brother proceeded to follow the course of the stream. All went well at first. From my place of concealment I saw him put up two or three Sandpipers, which came shrieking along straight for my ambuscade. But, alas! Fate was once more against us, and a single bird rising inopportunely from a ditch at right angles to the drain, and catching sight of me as it flew towards the estuary, uttered the now well-known warning cry, and in a moment my approaching victims had grasped the situation and swerved off rapidly to right and left.

Thus the drive, too, had proved a failure, and nothing remained but to wait for some hours in the harbour until the birds had had time to return. However, the collecting mania is not easily damped. We decided to wait, and, returning late in the afternoon, at length secured a specimen after an arduous stalk. We did this by making short semicircles, and then crawling straight towards the likely spots. To follow the drain was hopeless—it swarmed with Common Sandpipers, which invariably gave the alarm, and Green Sandpipers are not the sort to neglect a warning. The reputation they acquired on that day for wariness they have ever since retained, and though I have shot them since in other localities, it will be long ere I forget the excitement of that first and most irritating pursuit. The Common Sandpipers, on the contrary, flew on before us from corner to corner, sometimes stopping to dance and flirt their tails on one of the cross fences, and allowing a near approach as they found themselves unmolested by the gun.

The place might well have provided Wood-Sandpipers as well, but we never saw or heard of any being found there. The rough herbage which adorned the banks was frequented by several members of the Warbler genus, and looked very suggestive of Crakes. The bushes were the regular resort of Red-backed Shrikes, and Turtle-Doves were to be found in nearly all the larger trees. Ducks sometimes came there in the evening, and an occasional laggard lay up for the day in the clump of reeds at its mouth; but, on the whole, it was a typical haunt of Sandpipers, especially, I consider, of the "Green."

Birds like the Phalaropes and Temminck's Stint are more often to be met with at the brackish pools which lie just beside the turf sea-wall. Many are fringed with reeds, and present cover sufficient for a Duck, or

A LIKELY POOL.

even a wandering Bittern; and as they in places follow one another at intervals for a distance of several miles, they will well repay a careful examination, especially if the shooter advance along the outer side of the bank, and send a dog to explore the pools themselves. Coots, too, will sometimes take up their abode amongst the reeds, and Moorhens are almost always to be seen.

If the land be less thoroughly drained, and the pools more numerous, they develop at times into a regular marsh, as in the case of Thorpe Mere, at Aldeburgh. On these brackish meres some of the choicest Waders are to be met with. Here one may look with some confidence for the Dusky Redshank, a bird which I have only been able to recognize on the wing by its triple note, "too—too—too," uttered more slowly than that of the Green-shank. More silent, and less fidgety than its congener, it is not often to be observed upon the open shore. It may, indeed, once in a way be found in a tidal drain amidst the saltings, but the majority fly beyond the sea-wall to the fresh-water marsh, and on its open expanse they are, especially when associating with Greenshanks, most difficult birds to approach. It was here, too, that I had the good fortune to secure a Pectoral Sandpiper (*Tringa maculata*). It rose, with the dash of a Snipe, from a solitary tussock on the mere, and though mingling at once with a flock of Dunlin which happened to be passing, it was distinguishable even then by its darker colours and longer wings. Thrice it took part in their aerial evolutions, and then it left them and flew round and round in narrowing circles until it pitched again upon the original spot. I failed to get it at the time, but when I went straight to the same tussock on the following morning, it rose to an easy shot, uttering as it did so a curious double note—"chup, chup." Mr. D. G. Elliot, in his 'North American Shore Birds,' gives a most interesting account of the behaviour of this bird at its breeding haunts in the Yukon Valley. After the manner of the Grouse tribe, it can in the spring extend its throat to an enormous size, and thus adorned it makes play for the edification of its mate.

Avocets have been seen on the same mere, and also Wood Sandpipers and Temmincks, and though these localities are soon shot out, and often hold nothing at all, yet if there are any of the very rare Waders about it is generally here that they are to be met with.

E. C. ARNOLD DEL.]

[WEST NEWMAN.

THE PECTORAL SANDPIPER'S COURTSHIP.

CHAPTER XII.

THE WINCHESTER WATER MEADOWS.

THE stretch of meadow-land which runs from Winchester to Eastleigh has been regarded as a happy hunting-ground by myself and my brothers from the very earliest days of our collection. Few, indeed, must be the fields which have not listened to the twang of my catapult or the sharp crack of the walking-stick gun. And, in truth, none could desire a more perfect haunt for small birds. Lying, as they do, along the course of the Itchen, between two chains of downs, these meadows attract not only the water birds and Warblers, but other species also that one associates more readily with the upland heights. I have more than once seen Wheatears close to the river, while Stonechats and Whinchats are common near the canal below St. Catherine's Hill, and breed in the small plantations on its banks. It is in spring that these meadows are most enticing. Their sheltered dips and tangled hedges appeal with special force to the Warblers newly arrived from the south, and it is here that one listens, and not in vain, for the earliest notes of the summer birds. March brings us the welcome form of the Chiffchaff— the delicate harbinger of spring. Like the sturdier Wheatear, it never fails to brave the blustering winds; indeed, I met one once near Twyford in the middle of December. Tame as can be when they first arrive in small flocks of half a dozen, they soon separate and betake themselves to the tree tops, and then, for Warblers, they are hard to approach. The Chiffchaff may be observed in the very first meadow beyond the Warden's garden, and here, too, I have once seen the Greater Spotted Woodpecker, while the College bathing-place in the same field is one of the favourite haunts of the Kingfisher, our loveliest and most typical bird.

All the way down the valley the Kingfisher may be met with, sometimes chasing its mate with shrill cries across the pastures, sometimes sitting on the small arches which span the lesser streams; but, bright though it is, it often flies off without attracting observation, and it is perhaps most generally recognized by its note. I found the nest once, on April 17th, in a bank beside one of the small waterfalls beyond Twyford; it contained four eggs,

quite fresh, and laid on fish-bones. I could often in the winter have killed
it when Snipe shooting below St. Catherine's Hill, and have watched it there
taking headers after the smaller fish, and there is a garden near St. Cross
which has, I am afraid, witnessed the slaughter of many of these most
beautiful birds.   Still, though more frequent in some years than others, it
appears on the whole to hold its own, and as in some portions of the district
it is rigorously protected by the landowners, there seems no immediate
probability of the local race becoming extinct.

Many and varied are the localities where one may admire this skilled
exponent of the gentle art. I have watched him darting along the Sussex
estuaries, and fishing from the sluice gates, which shut off the salt water
from the meadows. I have watched him in Norfolk, perched on posts amidst
the saltings, or hovering at even above some tiny broad, poised on beating
wings like a humming-bird, a shimmering blaze of turquoise amidst the
crimson glories of the setting sun. Or, again, beneath Beachy Head I have
seen him sitting upon the rocks, diving at intervals into the pools left beneath them by the receding tide. But it is, nevertheless, with the southern
chalk streams that one instinctively associates the bird ; never does he seem
so much at home and in harmony with his surroundings as when seated on the
decaying stump of his favourite willow, or skimming across the eddying
river to the bank which he has chosen for his nest.

As we draw near to Twyford we keep a sharp look out for that
interesting bird the Hawfinch. The large, solitary may-bushes which stand
out here and there in the open provide just the sort of perch that the
Hawfinch loves. Here, on the topmost twig, he sits, an ever-watchful
sentinel, and almost as soon as you enter the meadow he has taken wing
and retired to some more secure retreat. It was long before I discovered
that the bird was to be found here at all ; and it was only the existence of
some peas in a garden near Twyford that at length brought it into
prominence, its partiality for this vegetable overcoming for a time its love
of seclusion and quiet. Once found and suspected of being a regular
denizen, I soon hunted out its more favoured haunts, and discovered that
in the large meadows beyond Twyford, and also amongst the yew trees
which adorn the hedges on the Shawford Down, the bird is to be met with
at all seasons of the year. I have little doubt that it breeds in some of
these fine old bushes, but have never had the chance of hunting at the
right season for its nest. Shy bird though the Hawfinch is, the conspicuous
light bar on the wings and its largish size make it easy to recognize, if
one is always on the look out, and able to tell birds at a distance. It is the

silent, unobtrusive way in which it decamps before you get near it that causes it to be so often overlooked.

As April advances, we hear the strange and unmistakable note of the Wryneck. But for its call, the bird, though not exactly shy, would often escape detection, owing to its skulking habits and the sober colour of its dress. As it flies along a hedge it might sometimes be mistaken for

IN THE TRIANGULAR MEADOW.

a dull hen Yellowhammer or Cirl-Bunting, but the dark chocolate triangle on the shoulders will always make identification easy, if one can once get a clear view of the back. Though it is most often found hopping clumsily about a hedge, or creeping up a branch, somewhat after the manner of a Woodpecker, the Wryneck can perch easily enough when it chooses, and I once watched one seated on a smooth, thin piece of wire fencing, where it seemed to retain its balance without any suggestion of its being a gymnastic feat. Towards the middle of the month the numbers of the other migrants begin to swell, and now is the time to visit that most charming of all the charming spots round Twyford—the triangular meadow at the end of the ruined wall. The place is a veritable bird paradise, and, indeed, within two hundred yards of its centre I have observed every species of bird that is to be met with in the meadows, save only the Green Sandpiper—a very rare visitant, which I have seen once beside the river, on the far side of the village. It is no wonder that the spot is such a favoured one. Surrounded on every side by water, the base is fringed with an osier bed, the natural domain of numerous Reed and Sedge-Warblers; and in the same shelter the Reed-Bunting also builds her nest.

Seated on a convenient stile, I have often looked in vain for the Marsh-Warbler, not without some faint hopes, too, of an Aquatic, but so far I have never had reason to suspect the presence of either bird. Once, at least, has this osier bed re-echoed the " chirring " note of the Grasshopper-Warbler, and on another occasion I followed the bird some distance along a neighbouring hedge, and noted especially the mouse-like creeping so often referred to in the books. The bird appeared much less rufous than the other Warblers—dark, but bright yellow olive, I should have called it, while a further means of identification was the absence of any distinct stripe above the eye. I have also met the Grasshopper-Warbler twice much nearer Winchester, and again near the large river beyond Twyford; and I believe that it breeds, though sparingly, in some of the dense undergrowth with which these meadows abound. I once had the chance of watching this Warbler's vocal efforts from a few yards off with glasses, and it was a strange sight indeed. The mandibles were kept wide open and motionless, the tongue appeared to be motionless also, though it may have been moving too quickly for the eye to follow. The " chirr " was very faint to begin with, and seemed to start in the pit of the stomach and to increase in volume as it worked upwards. It struck me that this comparatively sudden change from a low note to a loud one may perhaps have given rise to the oft-stated theory that the bird is possessed of ventriloquial powers.

At the back of the osier bed runs the river, and a small waterfall hard by is a great place for all the common Wagtails, and more than once I have seen a Sandpiper running nimbly about on the mass of decaying water-plants which is usually floating at its foot. On the banks of the two streams which bound the other sides of the meadow there is a fine combination of trees and bushes. The former can nearly always produce a Creeper and some Flycatchers, and not seldom a Wryneck or Nuthatch, while the Green and Greater Spotted Woodpeckers have been known to visit them at times, and once in winter I came upon a Great Grey Shrike. Rarely is the note of the Cuckoo wanting in the season, and amongst the numerous nests that are built here it must find a ready receptacle for its eggs.

At the apex of the triangle the stream broadens out, and forms a natural bathing-place for all the birds of the neighbourhood, and at this shallow pool I have seen in one morning all the common Finches, including the Hawfinch and Goldfinch, together with various Larks, Buntings, Marsh-Tits and others, Thrushes, and Warblers. The lane that leads down to the water

THE HOME OF THE KINGFISHER.

provides cover for all the less aquatic species of Warblers. The Lesser Whitethroat is here a comparatively common bird; so is the Garden-Warbler. The Common Whitethroat and Willow-Wren are everywhere, and the ivy berries which grow in such profusion on the old wall are almost sure to attract the Blackcaps when they first arrive. The statement that Nightingales and Blackcaps are seldom found in the same locality is here proved partially true, for though the Nightingale's song is heard directly you get to the west of the railway, I have only once seen the bird on the east of the bank, and it is on this side that the Blackcap is generally to be found. The Redstart, like the Nightingale, is more frequent as we approach the higher ground, but it, too, at times descends into the meadows.

Leaving the charmed precincts of the triangular meadow, we pass to the open fields around. Here breed the Lapwings in abundance, and occasionally a Wild Duck's nest may be found beside the river's bank. Corncrakes, Water-Rails, Moorhens, and Dabchicks are common, and I have flushed the Snipe late in April, though I have never succeeded in finding its nest. But perhaps enough has been said to indicate the wonderful variety of bird life that is to be seen here; in fact, on a bright spring morning few, if any, inland-walks can offer attractions to surpass those of the Itchen Valley, where ear and eye alike drink in the beauties of the scene, where the bleating of the lambs is mingled with the varied music of the birds, and the tender green of the willows is reflected in the silver mirror of the stream.

CHAPTER XIII.

DARTMOOR.

MOST people have a general idea that there is good fishing and excellent scenery to be met with on Dartmoor. Its wild tors and rocky glens appear without fail in every collection of photographs. Pictures of Holne Chase and the Buckland drives form an inseparable adjunct to all guides to Devonshire, and everyone has heard of its wild cattle and wild ponies. Lastly, there are few after-dinner conversations amongst members of the angling fraternity in which the waters of the Dart and its tributaries do not meet with frequent and well-merited eulogiums.

Many, however, are doubtless not aware that for the small sum of ten shillings a licence can be obtained, which enables the holder to shoot over the unenclosed parts of the moor, and a short description of the birds to be met with, and the places they frequent, may perhaps be of interest to the numerous class of sportsmen who can put up with a small bag gained by a good day's tramp over rough country. A zigzag railway from Yelverton, which dodges backwards and forwards among the tors so sharply that passengers in the last carriage can almost ogle the occupants of the first, lands one, probably about eight o'clock in the evening, at the station of Princetown, a village which owes its existence to the convict prison situated on the adjoining hill.

After being carefully scrutinized by some of its officials, the visitor must now choose between putting up at the Duchy Hotel, or driving one and a half miles onwards to Two Bridges, where excellent accommodation can also be obtained on the very bank of the East Dart. The latter hostelry will naturally commend itself to the angler, while Princetown is more convenient for the shooter, who could, moreover, at the Duchy obtain the aid of a thoroughly trustworthy setter, and a setter is a *sine qua non* on Dartmoor. The next thing is to procure a licence. This is granted by the bailiff of Dartmoor, who lives close by at Tor Royal, and gives permission to shoot anything except hares and Grey Hen within certain roughly defined boundaries included under the term " unenclosed lands in the Forest and

Chace of Dartmoor." Armed with this document, and happy in the acquisition of the aforementioned setter, the sportsman retires to rest with the
intention of opening the campaign against the Snipe on the morrow.

September 1st is the day on which all shooting begins, or rather should
begin, in this district, and, quite apart from winter visitants, good sport may
be had in that month amongst the home-bred contingent in the mires. Of
these, Fox Tor Mire is far the most famous. Distant about two miles, as
the crow flies, from Tor Royal, it is easy to find in broad daylight, and as
we had inspected the spot from a distance on the previous day, we had little
fear of being unable to find it on the succeeding morning; the only question
was whether we could be first upon the scene. But, alas! we had failed
to take into account one most important element in all sport on Dartmoor—
the mist! At five o'clock the men and the dog were up and ready to start,
but a dense mist covered the whole country with its impenetrable shroud.
Under the circumstances it was, of course, folly to start, but as the natives
confidently prophesied that it would lift, we set forth, quickly lost the way,
and marched grimly about the moor for nearly two hours in the wrong
direction. Then the mist did lift; we found a cottage, and were directed once
more to the mire, said to be then five miles off. We could at all events
plume ourselves on having avoided the inevitable circle. There was now
little difficulty in discovering the way, more especially as we were aided in
our search by the constant report of a gun, and in the end we arrived upon
the ground in time to congratulate another sportsman, who had worked it
thoroughly, and bagged eight and a half couple; we ourselves got one Teal.

Dennabridge Mire is the next best place for Snipe, which are, of course,
the most numerous game birds on the moor, but the greatest prize is the
Blackcock. Though not really uncommon within the Duchy shooting rights,
they are, nevertheless, very hard to obtain, chiefly, I believe, owing to the
fact that they are poached and persecuted before the season proper begins,
and consequently by the 1st of September it is a difficult matter to get near
them. Be that as it may, they frequent mostly those hillsides where the
heather mingles with long ruddy grass, and there are often some on a piece
of ground answering to this description on the south-east of Fox Tor Mire.
A second favourite haunt is the stretch of moorland between Two Bridges
and Great Mis Tor. Here, again, the heather is high and in clumps, and
the same sort of grass grows amongst it. Black-game may not be killed
after December 10th.

Beside the Blackcock, one occasionally meets with a covey of Partridges
or a Landrail. Such is the shooting which may be had on Dartmoor in

September; uncertain it must be admitted, but exciting at times, and always healthy and invigorating, for there is no denying the sustaining power of the moorland air. The walking in the mires is execrable; one false step, and you are up to your waist in liquid peat.

Two Bridges, where you get a licence to fish on the Dart and a trespass ticket for six shillings and sixpence, is the better centre for fishing operations, but even here, in September, the angler may be disappointed by the distance

THE DART.

he has to go for sport. When we visited it, the river was partially dry, and we had to walk or drive beyond Dennabridge before there was any really good water. Under the circumstances, Postbridge appeared in many respects a more desirable abode, but it is four miles further on towards Chagford, and doubtless the fishing round Two Bridges is good enough at other times. The trout as a rule are small, a half-pound fish being a good one. We heard of one being caught which weighed one and a half pounds. Despite the fact that the event was chronicled in the local papers, the captor boldly raised its weight to two pounds eight ounces within the week. Verily the licence allowed to anglers is more illimitable than that of poets!

Good fishing is always to be had from Dennabridge onwards to the Dartmeet, where the beauty of the scenery is proverbial. Besides trout and samlet, fair-sized peel are frequently captured in the evening, and another well-known denizen of the stream is the otter. I had the good fortune to watch one sporting for some time amidst the rapids below Wistman's Wood. There are not many species of the smaller birds to be met with, though Larks, Pipits, and Wheatears abound, and the Dipper "flaunts his white waistcoat" beside nearly all the swift-running streams. According to Morris, most of the rare Hawks have been secured in the neighbourhood, and the Buzzard is said to breed there still, but though Kestrels were quite common we ourselves saw none of the larger species.

On Sunday morning it is possible to obtain admission to the Convict Chapel, where about seven hundred prisoners assemble, and the effect of the men's voices in the hymns is most impressive. The hills of Dartmoor have ere now echoed back other shots than those of the sportsman, and time was when three of these unfortunates were shot in one morning while trying to escape. Of another it is told that, having eloped during an opportune mist, he spent the night in running before the wind, which shifted steadily, and landed him at daybreak within four hundred yards of the prison.

The subjoined Latin elegy, culled from the golden treasury of a cottage visitors' book, gives a not altogether untrue summary of the sporting capabilities of the neighbourhood. Can we suppose that the use of the perfect *genuit* in the eighth line suggests the ill-natured cynicism of some disgusted angler, who had toiled in vain for anything larger than a six-inch fish, the smallest size at which they can legally be transferred to the creel? If so, we think others may be found to sympathize, though perhaps unjustly, with his plaint. In any case, we can appreciate the monotonous jingle of the closing line, in which the poet does justice to the vapours characteristic of the locality, for Dartmoor is pre-eminently the land of fogs. Below we give the lines for what they are worth.

Carcer ubi triplex nebulosis montibus exstat,
    Copia venandi est, quaerite si quis amat.
Hic si forte juvat scolopacem figere telis
    dis horrenda palus Foxtoriensis adest,
Sed cave ne scolopax fallat te gurgite captum
    dum miser obscoenos fundis ab ore modos.
Squamigeram calatho si cura est cogere praedam,
    ingentes genuit Dartia Salmonidas.
Haec tibi contingent interdum, numine fausto,
    omnibus omnitegens tempus in omne vapor.

E. C. ARNOLD DEL.]

[WERT NEWMAN

LITTLE GULL (*immature*).

CHAPTER XIV.

THE OPEN SEA IN WINTER.

FEW strangers visit the open coast of Norfolk in the winter for shooting purposes, though the harbours of Lynn and Wells may boast of punts, punt-guns, and all the remaining paraphernalia of the wild-fowler. The reason is not far to seek. The shore-shooter of September, who lightly tramps his twelve or fifteen miles with the certainty of getting shots at Curlew, Red-shanks, Knots, Oystercatchers, and all the other shore birds which then frequent the sands and saltings, knows perfectly well that the best Waders are gone, and that such as remain, being now adults and collected in flocks, are under ordinary circumstances unapproachable; knows also that the journey to Norfolk is a long and uninteresting one, and has not unreasonable doubts concerning the style of food and lodging which await him at this season of the year. He therefore stays at home, and congratulates himself on his prescience in doing so—whether rightly or wrongly remains for the reader to decide.

Suppose some enthusiast to have survived the tedious journey in dimly lighted carriage from Liverpool Street; suppose that he has arisen uninjured from the clammy embrace of "well-aired" sheets, and triumphantly digested the supper of the preceding night : he sallies forth, not for a shoot along the shore, unless, indeed, mere exercise is his object, or unless he be a collector in pursuit of small birds. No; the man who means killing in the winter goes down to the nearest inn to find a boatman possessed of a flock of decoys. For the modest sum of five shillings, or thereabouts, he secures for the day the services of the local crack, and proceeds forthwith to the shore. On arriving there one is rather taken aback to see the boat floating at least a hundred yards off, and the tide still coming in. But your companion is equal to the occasion; a cheerful "with your leave, sir," and he has hoisted you on his back, and is tramping steadily through the water in his waders.

It should be said at once that the shooter ought to have an eight-bore at the least, and should take a twelve-bore as well for cripples. While your man rows you out two or three miles to sea, towards some well-known haunt, you ensconce yourself in the bows upon a heap of straw, and take your chance of a passing shot. Nor is this an unlikely contingency. Divers of various sorts, Guillemots, Razorbills, and Grebes all frequent this coast in the winter, and a collector may well make some valuable addition to his museum, though it is generally a case of kill dead or lose altogether, for chasing a wounded Diver seldom brings it to bag, and exhausts not only your own good temper, but, what it is far more important to husband, the energies of your rower.

Sometimes, too, a small flock of Duck may be seen floating in the distance, and a long shot be obtained. But, on the whole, it pays better to make straight for the place where the decoys are to be put down. This is often the mouth of an open bay, and if other shooters are about all the better; they will serve to keep the Duck on the move, and upon this depends the amount of sport to be met with. It is, in fact, a good plan to arrange that one boat shall act as driver, and keep well out to sea. The decoys are now anchored, and we both crouch down amidst the straw. As soon as the birds are put up, the men in the various boats begin to whistle, each trying to attract them to their decoys.

The Duck—which are mostly, but not all, Common Scoters (Black Duck, the natives call them, though the epithet is applicable only to the adult males, females and immature birds being dark brown with greyish breast)— seldom fail to see the dummies. Quite ignoring the presence of the boat, they sweep on in splendid style straight for the guns; fifty, forty, thirty yards only separate us now ; can they be coming right over ? No, they have at last seen through the trick, and in a moment they swerve abruptly to right and left. The measured sweep is exchanged for a series of short, rapid beats, and some most exciting shots are then obtainable, though, owing to the rocking of the boat, and the awkward attitudes in which the shooters are placed, the whole flock often passes by unscathed, and proceeds towards another party, to run the gauntlet of a second fusillade.

If any birds have been wounded—and the Scoter takes a hard knock to settle it—they dive immediately, and come up well out of range. Such as are only slightly damaged are most difficult to secure, and if you happen to miss seeing them when they first come up, it is long odds against your ever getting near them afterwards. It is therefore worth remembering that they usually collect together towards the close of the day, and a second attempt should then be made to despatch them.

Under favourable circumstances, and with a boat to drive, eight shots an hour is a fair average, but one local shooter is said to have bagged over sixty in the day. In fact, the attraction of the decoys appears quite irresistible both to the Ducks and others—or rather, another, for it happened in this wise. We were lying one day the middle boat of three, and D——, an old college friend, was out at sea driving. The man on the left winged a Scoter, which dived and tempted him to pursue it, leaving his decoys at anchor. Meanwhile D—— had grown tired of driving, and started in to suggest a change. On the way he espied the wanderer's decoys, eased promptly, and in another moment had solemnly begun to stalk them. We saw him crouch lower in the boat, while the oars dipped more slowly, more cautiously at every stroke.

He was now within fifty yards, and raised his gun; another stroke, and we could picture the grim look of triumph as he reckoned that he was bound to get a shot. Of course we ought to have shouted; we ought, but we didn't—we watched. It would doubtless also have been more sporting of D—— if he had waited to let them rise; but no—there was a bang; the two nearest bobbed hurriedly beneath the surface, rose again, one of them minus its head, and mocked the astounded gunner to his face; while D——'s boatman, grasping the situation in a twinkling, wheeled round with a fiendish chuckle, and made straight off for the open sea. Here they confined their efforts to driving for the remainder of the day. We solaced D—— afterwards by telling him how, when the device was first introduced, the real birds would often settle down amongst the sham ones. And this is true, though one can hardly credit it, as the decoys are for the most part roughly shaped lumps of wood or cork, painted black, and leaded to keep them upright, and then tied at intervals along a strong piece of cord.

Most people continue shooting until three o'clock, when it is time to renew the chase of the cripples. They will be found collected on the outskirts of a largish flock towards the open sea. It is best to stand upright, with the gun ready at the shoulder, for they come up in such unexpected places, and dive again so rapidly, that it is quite a difficult matter to get a fair shot at them, and many a cartridge will be wasted in the attempt. At last, however, they have all turned breast upwards, and we direct our boat towards the shore, for evening is closing in, and we have no desire to pass the night upon a sandbank.

Unfortunately, the Scoter will never provide a dish for the gourmand. The natives, however, receive them gladly, and say that, if skinned and soaked in salt water they are well worth eating. You probably try them—once. There is a meaning smile on your landlady's face as she lifts the cover, and reveals to the expectant epicure two dark, mahogany-coloured carcasses; and though, when first they taste them, most persons say "really very fair," "much better than I expected," &c., we imagine this only means that they expected very little. Anyhow, the carver notices that no one comes for a second serving; the so-called bones on people's plates are for the most part invisible beneath a solid covering of meat, while the proposal to have another pair cooked has, we are told, never been known to find a seconder.

As a rule, the finest pair find their way into the hands of a taxidermist; the remainder are distributed throughout the village.

CHAPTER XV.

THE NEW FOREST.

LOOKING over notes connected with a series of visits to the New Forest, one cannot but be struck with the paucity of rare birds that one remembers there. No doubt, as is the case with the Broad district, a dweller in the neighbourhood will in the course of years meet with many interesting species, but the casual visitor, however sharp his eyes, however fervid his energy, is almost sure to come away disappointed. This is due to the nature of the country. The splendid and varied scenery of the Forest, the heather-clad heaths, the spongy bogs and alder brakes, and the majestic grandeur of its noble trees, seem to mark it out as the natural rendezvous of the very *élite* of bird society, and this is just the reason why one sees so little—it is too often a case of good birds or none at all.

The Beaulieu and Lyndhurst heaths are ideal places for Harriers, but once only has it been my good fortune to see them there. So it is with Mark Ash and Boldre Wood; every moment one expects to see a Honey-Buzzard, but the Harrier and the Buzzard are gone, and silence reigns in the district that once re-echoed with their cry; and thus it comes about that from most expeditions to the New Forest one returns having seen little more than can be observed during an everyday walk in any ordinary wood.

Still the glorious traditions and associations of the place will always attract the naturalist; he will never feel satisfied until he has been there; and a record of the experiences of one who has often himself been disappointed may perhaps serve as a guide to the more likely spots, and save the new-comer from many an unproductive tramp.

As regards the shooting, the Forest has been called the "Poor Sportsman's Paradise"; but though a licence to shoot over it can be obtained for the moderate sum of £15 or thereabouts, the restrictions are of such a nature that only residents are likely to avail themselves of the privilege. Most people will be content to regard it as a place where they must lay aside the gun, but can ramble and study nature unrestrained. It is useless to try and do the Forest in a single walk; it is best to split up its area into

G

two or three districts, and devote a day to each. Lyndhurst Road provides a natural and convenient starting point, and the country round is some of the prettiest and most interesting from a naturalist's point of view, especially in the month of May.

Turning off sharp to the left from the Lyndhurst Road, you are soon engaged in picking your way through the boggy turf, and at once recognize the fact that for all forest exploration the first essential is a good, sound pair of boots. As you enter the picturesque glade that lies in front of Ashurst Lodge, a yellow form flits hastily between the trees, and the ear is greeted with the well-known laughing cry of the Green Woodpecker. As might be expected, it is a common bird in the Forest, and the numerous decayed trees in this neighbourhood seem specially adapted for its nest. It was here that I first got a good view of the bird upon the ground, and was much struck with the similarity of its actions to those of a Common Starling strutting about upon a lawn.

Another tree bird that is sure to meet us soon is the Nuthatch; its metallic note can never be mistaken, and will at once enable us to detect its owner as he stands hammering with short but sturdy beak a nut that he has fixed in some crevice of the bark, or hanging head downwards to inspect us with saucy defiant stare. The Nuthatch is deservedly a favourite; he always seems so merry, even in the hardest of winters, and there is a charm also in the harmony of its soft grey plumage, set off by the dash of bright chestnut on the flank, and the dark streak beside the eye. Like those of the Woodpeckers, his nest is in these trees; I once found it in the very first tree facing the road, but the hole, going right into the heart of the trunk, was impervious to any weapon short of an axe. This nest had no mud round the entrance, and was far more like the nest of a Tit, but to judge by the bird's actions we can hardly have been mistaken as to the ownership. Another pair of Nuthatches that I knew of that season were not equally happy in their selection of a site. Long before May was in they had secured a hole in a small oak tree, and narrowed down the entrance with the usual wall of mud. A deep layer of oak leaves already lined the hollow, and everything was ready for the eggs. Some days later we went to look for them, but the first glance as we entered the clearing revealed the unwelcome fact that the mud wall was demolished. Burglars had evidently been at work; nay, one was still upon the premises, for as we advanced a head was thrust forth and hurriedly withdrawn into the hole. It was the work of a moment to clap a hand over it, and then, eager to find who the intruder might be, we lowered an extemporized noose into the hollow, and, after fishing for twenty minutes without success, at length hauled forth the piebald form of a Greater Spotted Woodpecker. The tree was one which swarmed with ants, and presumably the prospective convenience of possessing a larder ready at hand had proved too much for the moral scruples of *Dendrocopus major*, and in the subsequent struggle for possession the weaker competitors had gone to the wall. The following year the disputed property was again annexed by the Nuthatches, and there was also a second nest

CRAB WOOD.

within one hundred yards of the old one, this latter being, like the first, in an oak tree infested with ants. The Lesser Spotted Woodpecker I have never seen near Lyndhurst, but it is an easy bird to overlook, and the locality is well adapted to its requirements.

But perhaps, after all, the bird that one associates most closely with Lyndhurst is the Wood-Wren. Anywhere round Ashurst Lodge they may be met with, though the exact place seems to vary with each year. I had never seen a Wood-Wren till I met them here, and had often wondered

G 2

whether they would be easy to distinguish or not. A few seconds were sufficient to decide the point. The curious song and shimmering flight at once attracted the attention, while the greenish hue and broad yellow margins of the tertiaries made identification easy as soon as a nearer view was obtained. The first pair I saw were quite low down on small silver birches, but they are more often to be found in the beech and oak trees, dropping down with characteristic flight from the higher to the lower branches, sometimes even into a holly bush, but seldom, if ever, descending to the ground unless actually engaged in nest-building. The Wood-Wren is a most delightful little bird. Arriving late as it does—about the first week in May— it is seen when the spring foliage is at its best, and the New Forest has few more attractive sights to offer than these Ashurst glades, dotted here and there with bluebells and primroses, and above them the little Wood-Wren sporting amidst the delicate greenery of the budding trees. One other note that may be heard in this neighbourhood is that of the Wryneck, but the bird is now becoming more and more scarce, and is far less frequent than the Nuthatch.

South of Ashurst Lodge we come to that brown expanse of moorland called Matley Bog. On the heath itself, not very far from Lyndhurst Golf Links, I once saw two Hen-Harriers fluttering along at a safe distance from bush to bush, the light grey plumage of the male showing up well against the dark background of faded heather. They kept about one hundred yards off, and it seemed utterly impossible to get nearer. An alder brake in the centre of the bog is in spring the resort of a regular army of Warblers, which can be heard singing in every tree. I have, however, never come upon anything rarer than a Blackcap, though I once nearly trod upon a semi-albino Woodcock as it crouched in some dry leaves at the foot of a bush. The alders are very suggestive of Siskins, and, as Wise mentions them as occasional visitors to the Forest, they are probably to be found here at times. He speaks also of Dartford Warblers being observed amongst the Whinchats on Lyndhurst Heath, but the heath is now but sparsely covered with furze bushes, and though, with a bird of such skulking habits, certainty as to its absence is unattainable, I am inclined to think that the Dartfords have long since disappeared. If the explorer on his return to Lyndhurst Road finds that he has still some time to wait for his train, a visit to Costicle's Pond would be a good way of winding up the day. The pond lies a short distance down one of the woodland rides on the north side of the road. It is overgrown with herbage, but has the appearance of a good place, and one can well imagine some rarity occurring there. The surrounding woods are frequented by numerous members of the Crow tribe, and I have seen the Kingfisher darting along the small stream which traverses them.

After exploring the Lyndhurst neighbourhood, it will be well to turn one's attention to Beaulieu, and the famous river which runs thence into the Solent. Beaulieu is not an easy place to get at. You can either go to Beaulieu Road and walk three and a half miles across the heath, or take the boat to Hythe, which is five miles off along a similar road; but the

A WOODPECKER GLADE.

annoying thing is that, when you do get there, it is almost certain that you will be unable to secure a boat, and anyone who wishes to follow the river must do so by the primitive method of forcing a passage through the thickets which fringe the banks on either side. It is about nine miles to the river's mouth, and six miles thence along the Solent to Lymington; and allowing for the tiring nature of the walking, the person who starts from Beaulieu Road, and follows the above-mentioned route, will have had enough of it by the time the Lymington harbour appears in sight.

Many have gone into raptures over the beauty of the river, and if the
tide is high the scenery is picturesque in the extreme.   Owing to its winding
course and the way in which the woods slope down to the water, it hardly
looks like a river in many places, but gives the impression of a series of land-
locked lakes; while here and there some beautiful little creek shoots off into the
Forest, and, overgrown with reeds and water-plants at the further end, affords
a welcome resting place to the many Wild Fowl which are commonly to be
met with all along the river's length.   Hither, too, come the Herons from
Vinney Ridge, and, loth to leave these sequestered pools, they flap forth, time
after time, beneath the very nose of the intruder—the tamest race of Herons
that I have ever met with anywhere.

As we get nearer to the Solent, and meadows take the place of woodland
on the banks, we shall soon be listening to the shrill " peeweet " of the Lapwing, or the far-reaching double note of the Redshank, which is also found
in some numbers near the river's mouth.   No doubt in bygone days this was
one of the favourite resorts of the Harriers, but there are none to be seen here
now; and though Green Woodpeckers are common along the banks, and
Beaulieu is the only part of the Forest where I have ever heard the Lesser
Spotted, it is with Ducks and Waders that the district mostly abounds.
From the Coastguard station there is a good path along the Solent to
Lymington.   On one side is a furze-brake, on the other open marshes, where
the Lapwings breed, and the whole place is very lonely and deserted by
everything save the birds.   The Lymington mudflats have been immortalized
by Colonel Hawker as a wild-fowling station, but it is hardly the sort of
place for an amateur, professional night-punting being there the order of
the day.

A third day's tramp in the Forest should take the direction of Mark
Ash and Boldre Wood.   One cannot hold out any great hopes of meeting
with rarities; in fact, my own visits have, so far as birds are concerned, left
behind them only a vision of Tits and Wood-Pigeons; but here, nevertheless,
if anywhere, will one encounter the larger birds of prey.   In Mark Ash my
brother claims to have seen a Peregrine; it passed quite close to him as he
stood beneath a holly-bush taking shelter from an April shower, and on the
same day he heard numerous raptorial cries.   This, too, was the last resort
of the Honey-Buzzard, and in these lofty beeches it made its last attempts
to rear a brood.   Had there been more thick brushwood beneath, it would
have had a better chance, but the walking is everywhere easy, and it cannot
have been very difficult to discover the nest.   The place merits a visit, if
only as being the last haunt of this extraordinary bird, but the scenery is

also the most impressive in the whole Forest. Starting from that unique structure, the charcoal burner's hut, the path leads gradually upward until it culminates in a knoll adorned by a noble company of the very largest trees.

The effective grouping of these leviathans, the intense silence that surrounds them, the sensation of smallness caused by standing at their feet, combine, one and all, to inspire an eerie feeling in the mind of the most soulless of observers. One starts for the moment at the squawk of the Jay, or the roar of wings, as a hundred Pigeons dash across the highest tops ; even the note of the Tit seems to have lost its merriment amidst the sombre majesty of the grove.

Such is the New Forest, not remarkable, perhaps, for its list of rarities, nor even for the number of birds to be seen there, but a place where there are no trespass boards, where the inland naturalist can wander unrestrained,— one of those tracts, so rare in Southern England, where one can revel in that feeling of absolute freedom so seldom nowadays to be experienced, save on the boundless mudflats of the shore.

CHAPTER XVI.

THE OLD DECOY, EASTBOURNE.

EASTBOURNE itself is hardly the place one would select for the study of ornithology, though I have known a Red-legged Partridge captured in the College football-field, and seen a Kestrel hovering over it, and a Nightjar fly down Blackwater Road. A Goldfinch, too, was slain with a brick in Carlisle Road, and Wood-Pigeons breed freely in some of the gardens round the Devonshire Park. To one, however, who is desirous of going further afield, there is no lack of interesting places in the neighbourhood.

In former times the most popular of these places was the Decoy Wood at Willingdon, more familiarly known as "The Decoy." This delightful piece of marshy woodland is now transformed into a public park; but though the naturalist will fain cry "Ichabod" when he visits it, a short description of its former glories may perhaps on that account be all the more welcome if it catches the eyes of any who happen to have been at school at Eastbourne, and to have known the Decoy in its palmy days.

You entered the Decoy by one of the numerous gaps in the hedge, and found yourself at once in a species of small birds' paradise, the equal of which I have never seen elsewhere. Timber of all sorts abounded, from the tall elms of the extensive rookery to the delicate sallow and hazel bushes, where the Nightingale concealed her nest. The first patch of brambles was almost sure to produce something, perhaps a Blackcap's or a Whitethroat's nest, and then we stumble on a disused Wren's nest hidden away amidst the moss and ivy that garnish a decaying stump. One always seems to find three abandoned Wrens' nests for every one with eggs, so fastidious or suspicious is the architect of these domed abodes.

As we get deeper into the thicket, the melodious note of the Nightingale breaks upon the ear. One's first Nightingale's eggs—how every schoolboy longs to find them! How many are the tiring and exasperating hunts among the herbage, while the male bird does his best to muddle you by singing desperately in the adjoining brake. But at last they are found; our hands, torn by thorns and stung by nettles, have pushed aside the fragile covering, and at the foot of some hazel or sallow bush there lie revealed at length those pale brown eggs. Near Cambridge I once found a clutch dark green with reddish flecks, but these, which are supposed to be laid by birds that return to the same spot every year, though a very beautiful variety, are far less typical than the pale brown egg. What always strikes one about subsequent Nightingales' nests is the ease with which they can be found. How was it, we wonder, that I never got one before? The fact is, finding them is less a matter of keen sight than experience. The novice is nowhere beside the old hand. But in any case it was a tiring job bending in the search, and one gladly returned after it to the heap of cut sedge and wood shavings that used to lie beside a tumble-down shanty on the eastern edge of the Decoy.

It was a likely spot for a Creeper's nest, or, later on in the season, for a Flycatcher's. Here one could listen to the soft note of the Cuckoos, which could here have had little difficulty in discovering a suitable resting place for their eggs. Ten feet up yon fir tree a Wood-Pigeon is sitting on her snow-white eggs, and a Sparrowhawk's eggs have been taken quite unexpectedly from a nest no farther from the ground.

I was always on the look-out for two birds which ought to have been present—the Grasshopper and the Marsh-Warbler. The former one could hardly have overlooked, owing to its striking note, but, though some of the tussocks would have formed an admirable receptacle for its nest, I looked in vain for it year after year. Breeding later, as the Marsh-Warbler does, it may well have escaped observation, owing to the density of the foliage after the month of May; moreover, I am unacquainted with its note, which would probably be the only means of recognizing it.

We once worked up a fine flutter of excitement over a pseudo-Orphean's nest. A curious damaged egg was brought me by a boy, who had taken it with two others from the Decoy. Ignorant of their value, he had been induced to exchange these latter—on paper a very bad bargain—with a local naturalist, who afterwards proclaimed them the eggs of an Orphean Warbler. The man affirmed that he had found the nest there himself the preceding spring, and was sure of their identity, for he had compared them with undoubted specimens at a well-known London naturalist's, of which his shop was a branch. Though not much impressed by the information, I was sufficiently stirred by the oddness of the egg to enquire if the bird had been seen, and I was all excitement a few minutes later, when I heard it described as "greyish, with a black head and white in the tail." Here was indeed a find, and I had visions of writing to the 'Zoologist,' and inviting down some distinguished authority to study the breeding of the Orphean Warbler in England.

The following day I was off to the Decoy with field-glasses, and, accompanied by the finder of the nest, who was fully persuaded that he was going to acquire undying fame in the highest ornithological circles, I made my way to the distinguished visitors' retreat. I may mention that two eggs had been left in the nest, so that there was a reasonable chance of finding the birds still there. The first sight of the nest was not encouraging; it was close against the main stem of a small-tree, and strongly suggestive of a Finch's. However, up we climbed, and found that it contained two fledglings. So far so good; identification of some sort was now assured. I sent off my guide to hunt for further rarities, and sat down behind a bush with my glasses. And now occurred jar number one. I had not been there five minutes, when a well-known note came echoing through the wood, and a Great Tit settled in the tree above my head. The black head, grey body legend was explained; the Orphean was fast receding into space. Still, the nest could not be a Tit's anyway, so I sat on with a pretty solid foreboding of what the end would be. It came, as I expected, in the shape of a female Chaffinch, with a caterpillar in her beak, which she shortly transferred to the expectant youngsters in the nest.

The Orphean myth was now exploded, and with it departed out short-lived hopes of ornithological renown. The only consolation was that the professional had come second best out of the bargain after all. I could not resist the temptation of calling on him to see what had become of the remaining eggs. I found him jubilant over the transaction; they had been despatched with the utmost care to London. He repelled with vigour an insinuation that they were not Orphean's after all, and implied pretty clearly that I was a fool; but mine, nevertheless, was the last word on the subject, when I suggested that in that case it was odd that a hen Chaffinch should be feeding the two remaining birds; and with this Parthian dart still rankling I left him to ruminate on his misdeeds.

To return to the Decoy itself. By the time a Nightingale's nest was discovered, we were generally pretty well seasoned to nettles, and, twisting a handkerchief round the hand that held the stick, we went straight for the nettle clumps themselves. They would always hold a Blackcap's or a Lesser Whitethroat's, and sometimes the rarer Garden-Warbler's was to be found in a similar position. Through the centre of the Decoy proper there flowed a narrow, reed-fringed stream, and this was an almost certain find for a Reed-Warbler's nest, while from the centre of the little decoy, which lay adjacent to it, I once put out the unlooked-for form of a fox! But alas! these days are gone for ever. The mongrel poodle has replaced the fox; Swans and barbarian Wild Fowl have ousted the native Duck, and pleasure parties daily disport themselves in what was once a naturalist's preserve.

CHAPTER XVII.

THE CRUMBLES.

THE study of ornithology may indeed be said to have been brought up-to-date when you can be transported to the scene of your researches in a motor 'bus! Yet to this climax of perfection has Eastbourne attained. Its motor 'bus will land you within five minutes' walk from the Crumbles— that is to say, within five minutes of one of the best hunting-grounds in the whole of the British Isles. I mean, of course, for rarities. Quality, not quantity, must be the motto of the shooter over the Crumbles. He must have realized that vast and crowded mudflats do not of necessity mean rare birds. He must be wedded to the cult of the odd corner, must be prepared to bring home his gun unused, and prepared also to level it at a moment's notice at almost any bird on the British list. I may add that the shooting over the Crumbles is not free, but is confined to a small party of about a dozen guns. To describe the place is almost to idealize the requirements of the collector.

You have, inside an hour's walk, a marsh with mud and reeds, shingle with brackish pools, and, surrounding the latter, bushes such as might shelter almost any Warbler under the sun. All this is found on a low-lying piece of ground, and above it a vast waste of shingle extends right away to Pevensey village, in the middle of the bay. It is not to be wondered at that with such variety of surface there is variety also to be met with amongst its birds.

Most of my earlier expeditions to the Crumbles were made in company with Mr. A. H. Streeten, then a boy at the College. They were made in search of eggs, and many most enjoyable afternoons did we have there. For two whole seasons we hunted, on an average once a week, for the nest of a Ringed Plover. Several pairs were breeding, but, though we found the young birds more than once, we never could light upon an egg. We could not even decide in our own minds whether the nests were on the lower plateau, or whether the birds hatched out up above, and then escorted the young ones down to the pools.

The following year Streeten's young brother had joined us, and we took him out to aid in the search. I expected him to dream most of the time, which he did; but I laughingly remarked, on the way out, that he would doubtless be the person to show us how to find Plovers' eggs. Of course he did it; he walked straight up to some on the side of a mound of shingle on the lower ground, and thereby settled the vexed question, so far as that pair was concerned. Having thus broken the spell, we found another nest the following year, also on the lower ground, and also on the side of a mound of stones, the theory that they lay just above high-water mark being rather exploded, so far as these nests were concerned. From this second nest we purposed only taking one egg; but, just as we were coming away, we noticed that we were being watched through glasses by two men lying upon the beach, and guessing that they would have the other eggs if we didn't, we ourselves annexed the clutch. We were quite right, for no sooner had we departed than they issued forth with a dog and went straight for the spot, where we soon saw the dog sniffing zealously at the empty nest.

I believe myself, though I have never proved it, that these Ringed Plovers breed on the shingle above as well. We have there found the nests of Lapwings, and also of Redshanks, which are here very easy to discover. The amount of grass suitable for making their arbour is so limited that it serves to attract you to the spot, but the birds themselves are as wily as ever. If you don't put them off the eggs they never fly near them while you are there, though they do sometimes utter a distant cry when you are getting quite close to the spot.

Further on towards Pevensey the Common Tern still breeds, but in diminishing numbers, while I have been shown undoubted eggs of the Dunlin, which bred on the Crumbles two years in succession. The most interesting of the small birds that nest there is the Yellow Wagtail. The pairs seem to have increased in numbers since I first noticed them, and as the nest is hard to find they may well continue to do so. The Blue-headed Wagtail has bred as near as Winchelsea, and I once thought I saw one on the Crumbles in the spring. I could not get near enough to identify it for certain, but the birds occur unquestionably in the autumn, the majority in immature plumage. Concerning this plumage, the books state that it is almost indistinguishable from that of the Common Yellow Wagtail, and no bird is accepted as a Blue-headed unless it has a perfectly white eye-stripe. As I once pointed out in the 'Zoologist,' I still believe that the immature Blue-headed has a darker, more olive-green back than the commoner bird. It is this feature that has always attracted my attention when I have shot them, and I would suggest that the young Blue-headed

E. C. ARNOLD DEL.I

WEST NEWMAN.

may well have a tinge of buff in its eye-stripe, just as the young Pied has a
tinge of lemon in places where the adult is white.

As regards the shooting capabilities of the Crumbles, as with the mere
at Aldeburgh and all small places, it is a case of first come first served. The
first arrival shoots the place out in an hour, and the next comer hardly fires
a shot. In fact, those who go there for sport, generally devote themselves
to the rabbits among the furze bushes; and the marsh, unless there happen
to be Duck or Snipe about, is handed over to the collector without regret.

THE HASSOCK.

And now what is there for him to get out of it? To start with, it is just
the place for the Dusky Redshank, the Greenshank, and the Wood-Sandpiper;
they have all been obtained there, together with the Green. I myself once
got a Red-necked Phalarope. It was scudding about, with true Phalarope
buoyancy, on the far side of the water, dodging in and out amidst the reeds,
and occasionally indulging in short flights, with a motion not unlike that
of a dragon-fly. It was so absurdly tame that when I first got over there
I positively passed it by, though only a few yards off. I have also met with
the Grey Phalarope once, and noticed that it swam lower in the water
than the Red-necked, and another rarity that has been shot there is the
Spotted Crake: and while I am on the subject of spotted creatures, I may
as well add that Mr. J. H. Gurney assured me that he has a Spotted

Sandpiper taken at the same place. Two other rarities have, to my know-ledge, been secured by College boys. In September, 1906, L. E. Dennys shot a Red-necked Phalarope, and in the same month G. H. Beattie obtained a Glossy Ibis with a small Winchester rifle. The last-named reached Mr. Bates in such an advanced stage of decomposition that I hardly expected him to stuff it. He managed it, however, and it is now in the Institute. Eastbourne seems to lie in the line of the Ibis migration, for two of these birds were obtained on Pevensey Marsh in the autumn of 1905.

The best birds that I have seen on the Crumbles myself have for the most part appeared in the close season, when I was without a gun. In June, 1902, I was attracted by the peculiar cry of a large Wader, which was flying about amongst some Redshanks. Its tail, doubtless owing to its long extended legs, appeared very triangular as it passed me, and the wings seemed to have a good deal of black in them. We thought it must be a Black-tailed Godwit, but, if so, its flight was much quicker than that of the Bar-tailed, and it did not seem quite large enough. I have since thought that it may have been a Stilt, but, owing to the light and the angle at which it always approached us, we found it impossible to get a good view. Anyhow, the size and note stamped it as a good bird, though more than that I am not prepared to affirm.

More certainty attaches to the identification of another queer bird which Streeten and I saw there on June 21st, 1903. When first observed, it was flying over the higher shingle, where some of the Ringed Plovers are to be found, and but for its peculiar flight, which was like a Nightjar's, it might perhaps have passed for one of these. The flight once noticed, we listened eagerly for the note. The bird soon uttered it, and there was no resemblance to that of a Plover. After watching it for some time, we decided that it must be a Pratincole, and further investigation on June 28th confirmed us in this surmise. The idea afterwards received unexpected support from the 'Zoologist,' wherein it was announced that a Pratincole had been shot at Rye on July 17th. As our bird was not seen again on the Crumbles, so far as I know, after the 28th, it is not unreasonable to suppose that in an ill-fated moment it had been inspired to move on to Rye. *Quem deus vult perdere prius dementat.*

I had another interesting day in the same July, when asked to show the Crumbles to a visitor who was fond of natural history. I told him when we started that he might see anything, and he replied that he would be quite satisfied with breeding Redshanks and Ringed Plover. These he saw and duly appreciated, also some Terns which were fishing in one of

the pools. We were lucky, too, in unearthing a young Lapwing, which feigned injury, and two young Ringed Plover, whose mother went through a performance that was new to both of us. She flew at a sloping bank of shingle just beyond the nestlings, and clung on to it with wings spread somewhat after the manner of a Woodpecker; it was an original, and certainly an effective, way of distracting our attention from the young birds.

But the *bonne bouche* was yet to come. Returning towards the marsh, we espied a small Wader, which I supposed at first to be a Little Stint,

THE CRUMBLE PONDS.

a bird which is regularly to be found there in the autumn. It proved, however, to be a Temminck, for we not only got a clear view of its colour, but when it got up it uttered the unmistakable trill which is always attributed to this bird in the books. Turning for a moment to the smaller birds, Streeten and I once identified a Bluethroat in September, and I have twice shot Blue-headed Wagtails from the flocks of the commoner species; but in dealing with the Warblers one is at a serious disadvantage, for disadvantages the Crumbles have; firstly, in the matter of the walking, which is over loose shingle; secondly, in the multitude of blackberries on the bushes. Blackberries mean blackberry-gatherers, and this, too, at the time of the autumnal migration; and believing, as I do, in the principle of not bringing home anything larger than one can conveniently carry, I have found it next to impossible to let off a gun at that season in the bushes, though I have not infrequently seen small birds that I failed to recognize, and at which I should much have liked to have a shot. I always went in hopes of picking up some rare Pipit at one of the pools, or perhaps a good Bunting from the small bushes in the open, but two whole seasons passed without my seeing anything that appeared worth shooting at. At last, on November 17th, 1905, a large dark Pipit flew across me, with a flight very dropping even for a Pipit. I secured it, and then noticed that the throat was very white, and the back distinctly brown without any olive tinge. The legs were stout and dark, and the soles of the feet were bright lemon. Lastly, though the light portion of the outer tail-feathers was not pure white, it was sufficiently near that colour to make me suspect that I had got a Water-Pipit. On the 25th I shot another similar bird, and on submitting one of them to an examination by Mr. Howard Saunders I found that my surmise had been correct. I have not yet got the rare Bunting, but Mr. Bates has, for a Lapland was brought him by a bird-catcher not long since, and he has also received a Shore-Lark from the same source.

In the winter, Geese sometimes pass over the Crumbles, and a fair sprinkling of Duck are to be met with if we get a snack of really cold weather. I have myself secured a Golden-Eye, and Mr. Bates has a Ferruginous Duck said to have been shot there. I have also seen a Great Crested Grebe on one of the lagoons, and a smaller Grebe on another. Herons from Hurstmonceux heronry are often to be found; Gulls are inevitables, and sometimes in winter I notice also the Hooded Crow. Lastly, I have Dr. Colegate's authority for stating that he once saw a Raven shot there in a dense fog.

CHAPTER XVIII.

SOME SOUTHERN CLIFFS.

PRE-EMINENT for grandeur among all our southern headlands stands the mighty precipice of Beachy Head, and after it I should place Culver Cliff, Freshwater, and the chalk cliff at Swanage. Before I first saw Beachy, it was always connected in my mind with Captain Knox's description of its Peregrines and Guillemots. It was therefore no small disappointment to discover that the Guillemots which used to breed there are extinct. One solitary bird, washed in by the sea one stormy October, and captured by Mr. Edelsten, is the only specimen of which I have any recent record.

What caused the Guillemots to forsake their ancient nesting-place I have never been able to discover, unless, indeed, the frequent landslips, to which the chalk is subject, have carried away the ledges on which they once deposited their eggs. The state of the cliff to-day is such that the Gulls can barely find sufficient projections for their wants, and there are certainly no long flat platforms such as a colony of Alcidæ would require. Myself, I live in hopes that they may yet return, if a convenient landslip will only provide them with a ledge; and there are rumours that odd pairs are seen at times in the breeding season.

But, after all, Beachy can afford to overlook the loss of its Guillemots so long as its Peregrines still remain. These glorious birds, despite incessant persecution, still retain possession of their ancestral domain, and no other bird, save perhaps the Eagle, could harmonize more thoroughly with the stupendous grandeur of this noble precipice, as seen from the shore below. I say the shore advisedly, for the view from the top gives no idea of its magnificence.

In May, 1904, a college boy named Morton asked me to look at three eggs, which he had taken from the Beachy cliffs. They were Peregrine's without a doubt, and, paradoxical as it may seem, he had done the race a real service by annexing them. The nest from which they came—in the previous year it had belonged to a Gull—was high up just over the edge of the cliff, and when he reached it the Falcon was on the eggs and a gin was

H

set quite close to her. The gin went over the cliffs and the eggs into Morton's pocket, and one can hardly doubt that but for this fact the bird would have eventually been caught on the nest, and, together with its eggs, have become the spoil of the unknown setter of the gin. As it was, the nest was sure to be deserted, and I went a few days later to see if I could get a glimpse of the birds. I had never seen any Peregrines alive, and I shall not readily forget this, my first view of them.

As we rounded a corner near the lighthouse the Tiercel, who was acting as sentinel, flew off the cliff about half-way up, and with shrill screams and rapid beats circled round us within easy range of a gun. Some seconds later the Falcon followed him, and for quite five minutes we enjoyed the splendid spectacle of a pair of Peregrines wheeling round our heads, mingling with, but apparently quite unnoticed by, a crowd of equally distracted Gulls, which were breeding hard by on the lower portion of the cliff. The Peregrines seemed this time to have selected a nesting-site quite unapproachable from either top or bottom. What struck me most about them was their tremendous wing power. They were not as large as I had expected, not looking any larger than Kestrels, but the breadth of wing across the secondaries was sufficient to distinguish them at a glance, even when high up and with their colours undiscernible. Their flight, too, was different: strong rapid beats propelled them through the air in a manner very unlike the indolent and erratic glide of the Kestrel. Their tails also appeared shorter, and, generally speaking, they were less elegant but sturdier birds—there was a sort of "rugger" build about them; they were of the type that goes through anything.

I went again, shortly afterwards, to have another inspection, but the whole place was bathed in sea fog, and as the coastguard was firing off a gun every five minutes for the guidance of passing ships, all the birds had been disturbed. We did see a Peregrine, nevertheless; high over our heads it passed out of the mist on one side, and was buried again in a few seconds on the other, but there was no mistaking the beat of its pinions, even in that deceptive light.

The final scene in the history of this attempt on the part of the Peregrines to bring off a brood at Beachy must, if I have been rightly informed, have been a dramatic one. Some unknown persecutor—perhaps the owner, or rather ex-owner, of the gin—set out in the early morning equipped with a gun, a Pigeon, and a string. Arrived opposite the eyrie, he loaded the gun, tied the string to the Pigeon's leg, and flew it temptingly before the face of the cliff. The answer to this challenge was instantaneous. The Peregrine stooped at it like a thunderbolt. The gunner lost his head, and hurriedly fired

[West Newman.

both barrels before it had struck the lure. He missed it clean and the
next thing he realized was that Peregrine, Pigeon, and string were careering
along in safety a quarter of a mile out at sea. As two Peregrines were
subsequently seen upon the downs escorting three young ones in the middle
of July, it is to be presumed that these much afflicted birds eluded to the end
all the efforts made to destroy them, and gained a well-earned triumph over
their foes.

With the Peregrines of Culver Cliff and Swanage I have been unlucky,
and, though I have reason to believe that they still frequent both these time-
honoured haunts, I have always had to content myself, so far as the Raptores
are concerned, with the contemplation of their feebler congener, the Kestrel.
It has been just the same with the Ravens; I have had to put up with the
Jackdaw, and have never come across a Raven outside Cornwall, but they
are, nevertheless, reported at times, by trustworthy witnesses, from Beachy
Head.

The birds that always present themselves in abundance, whichever cliffs
you visit, are the Herring-Gulls. The Beachy Head colony is distinguished
by the unusual simplicity of some of its members. It is now an open secret
among the boys of Eastbourne College that the Beachy Herring-Gulls frequently nest upon the ground! The youth who first discovered the fact
was known to be a good climber, and suspected of a distant connection with
Ananias. His return one day with a load of Gulls' eggs, and the announce-
ment that he had found them on the ground, merely confirmed his reputation
in both respects, and no one even took the trouble to go and test a statement
so obviously absurd.

Some years later several boys, starting on a Sabbath day's journey, which
proved most disastrous to the Gulls, re-discovered the secret, and I was myself
induced to go and have a look at the nests. Needless to say, those I saw
were empty, the majority being a few feet up the cliff amongst loose boulders,
though several were actually on the shingle just at its base. Further on,
near Birling Gap, I saw two Gulls right down on the shore just above high-
water mark, and suggested that perhaps they were breeding there. To our
amazement, when we reached the spot, there was the nest with two eggs in it.
It was mostly of straw, and had a large bit of red flannel woven into it. At
Culver Cliff and Swanage I have found these Gulls' nests quite low down, but
none of them positively on the ground.

From the foot of Beachy a reef of sunken rocks runs out to sea in a
slanting line, and at low tide I have shot the Purple Sandpiper at this point,
and heard of others being taken there. I also one day watched a Kingfisher

diving off these rocks into the little pools left by the receding tide. A Red-necked Grebe has been captured not far off, and one can always count on the presence of Rock-Pipits, Stonechats, and Wheatears in their season. I am told also that this portion of the cliffs is frequented at times by the Black Redstart, but I have once only had the luck to find it there myself.

The Guillemots, which ought to frequent Beachy, but don't, may be found at Swanage, if you go along the Durleston cliffs. From the top you can see both Guillemots and Puffins riding on the waves, and even at that distance you can distinguish the latter by the light colour of their cheeks. It is a strange sight to see these Guillemots leave their ledges. You throw a stone over the edge, and immediately out dash the birds, and, forming as they do into a wedge-shaped phalanx, almost mathematically correct, they have an odd, toy-soldier sort of appearance from above; one might almost think they were machines rather than birds. These Durleston cliffs are some of the wildest that I know of in the south. One felt that a Peregrine or Chough might turn up at any moment, but it was again a case of the Jackdaw and the Kestrel.

The chines that run down the cliffs on the Bournemouth side of Swanage are garnished with luxuriant and unusual vegetation. They are frequented by certain rare butterflies, and provide a perfect resting place for newly arrived Warblers from the south; but I think they lie outside the line of the main migration, and they actually held only a few Whitethroats and Willow-Wrens.

When I first sat down to write this chapter I had visions of including another most interesting bird amongst the denizens of my local cliff, and as a specimen of the way in which one may be deceived by what appears quite trust-worthy evidence, I will explain how nearly I came to crediting Beachy with the possession of two Choughs' nests as recently as 1904. In May of that year —in fact, the very day after Morton found the Peregrines' nest—another boy entered my study with some eggs in his hand which he had taken from a rabbit-hole on the cliff. He suggested that they were rather strange for Jackdaws', and thought perhaps they were Choughs'; I thought so too, though I had never seen a Chough's egg. Rarities often come in couples, and I seemed to scent another ornithological sensation. These eggs appeared rather more oval than those of a Jackdaw, the blue colour was very pale, and the spots small and very faint. The books tended to confirm our theory; but who ever got any positive information out of coloured plates of eggs? Thus matters remained *in ambiguo* for two days, when another boy walked into my class-room for me to pass judgment on some eggs. He opened a box, and I was almost dumbfounded to behold three precisely similar specimens! Had they seen the bird, was my prompt enquiry? "Yes; they had put it out of a hole in the cliff; black, with red legs and red beak." It seemed a clear case on the face of it, but I was eager to see for myself. Some days later I set out, but, though I walked to Birling Gap and scanned every sable form with the utmost care, there were no signs of a red beak, and I returned very much disappointed from my quest. Another visit was equally futile. A dense sea-fog came on, and though we went some way beyond Birling Gap we could not find a Chough. We came back along the top of the cliff, and there were dozens of Jackdaws feeding on the turf, but the fog prevented any comprehensive view, and was, generally speaking, so deceptive that the flocks—I was going to say herds—of Gulls seated on the grass looked almost as big as Geese; indeed, the mist was so solid that on a black coat it showed up white like hoar-frost. The eggs were then submitted to the scrutiny of the College Natural History Society, and the discussion that followed left us just as wise as we were before, the finder still grimly sticking to his red beak. Alas for juvenile confidence! When at length I got the chance of visiting the South Kensington Museum, our hopes were soon laid to rest. I found two Jackdaw's eggs exactly like ours, while the Chough's had a still lighter ground and much heavier blotches. So much for our attempt to resuscitate the Chough as a Sussex breeding species. Not that I have quite given up hope even now. I am informed by Mr. Bates that in December, 1905, a Chough was certainly seen on Pevensey Marsh. It was in the company of, or rather being mobbed by, some Rooks, a fact which first drew attention to its presence. The red beak and legs were then observed. Can it be that the Chough is now so utterly forgotten by the local Corvidæ that, when one does turn up amongst them, it is regarded as a monstrosity, and forthwith attacked as such?

CHAPTER XIX.

THE POLEGATE WOODS.

THE sylvan country, which is almost wanting at Eastbourne proper, can be found by making a short railway journey to Polegate. The woods round it are delightful; and as the birdsnester, who has tired himself out by hunting, can regale himself afterwards, in the village, on that very appropriate finale to a day's naturalizing, an egg tea, the locality has, since the desecration of the Decoy, been much frequented by the more energetic members of the Eastbourne schools.

A charming lane, though too often ankle-deep in mud, brings you to one of the best known woods, in the midst of a district which, as things go nowadays, is quite a stronghold of raptorial birds. Most of the Kestrels, it is true, frequent the neighbouring cliffs in the spring time, but some few breed in the woodlands, and the Sparrowhawk is here as common a bird as in any locality that I am acquainted with throughout the whole of the British Isles.

In the autumn of 1906, however, a far nobler member of the family was captured in one of these woods. A rustic wandering through them was astonished to see a large Hawk tearing up a wasps' nest in a bank. Not realizing that it belonged to a harmless species, he rushed home, secured two traps, and, returning, set one on each side of the nest. In a short time the bird, a male Honey-Buzzard, was caught; but the female, which was also seen, passed on unmolested.

This bird, after changing hands once, came into my possession, and is now in the Eastbourne Museum, having been admirably mounted by Mr. Bates. Concerning it a writer in 'The Field' of February 17th, 1906, Mr. H. A. Bryden, remarked:—

"Although called Honey-Buzzard, the bird is actually not a honey eater, but, like the Honey-Guide of South Africa, visits the nests of bees and wasps, and even of the formidable hornet, for the grubs found in the comb. The Honey-Guide, by the way, calls in the aid of man, while the Honey-Buzzard storms the nests and caters boldly for himself. It also devours the wasps

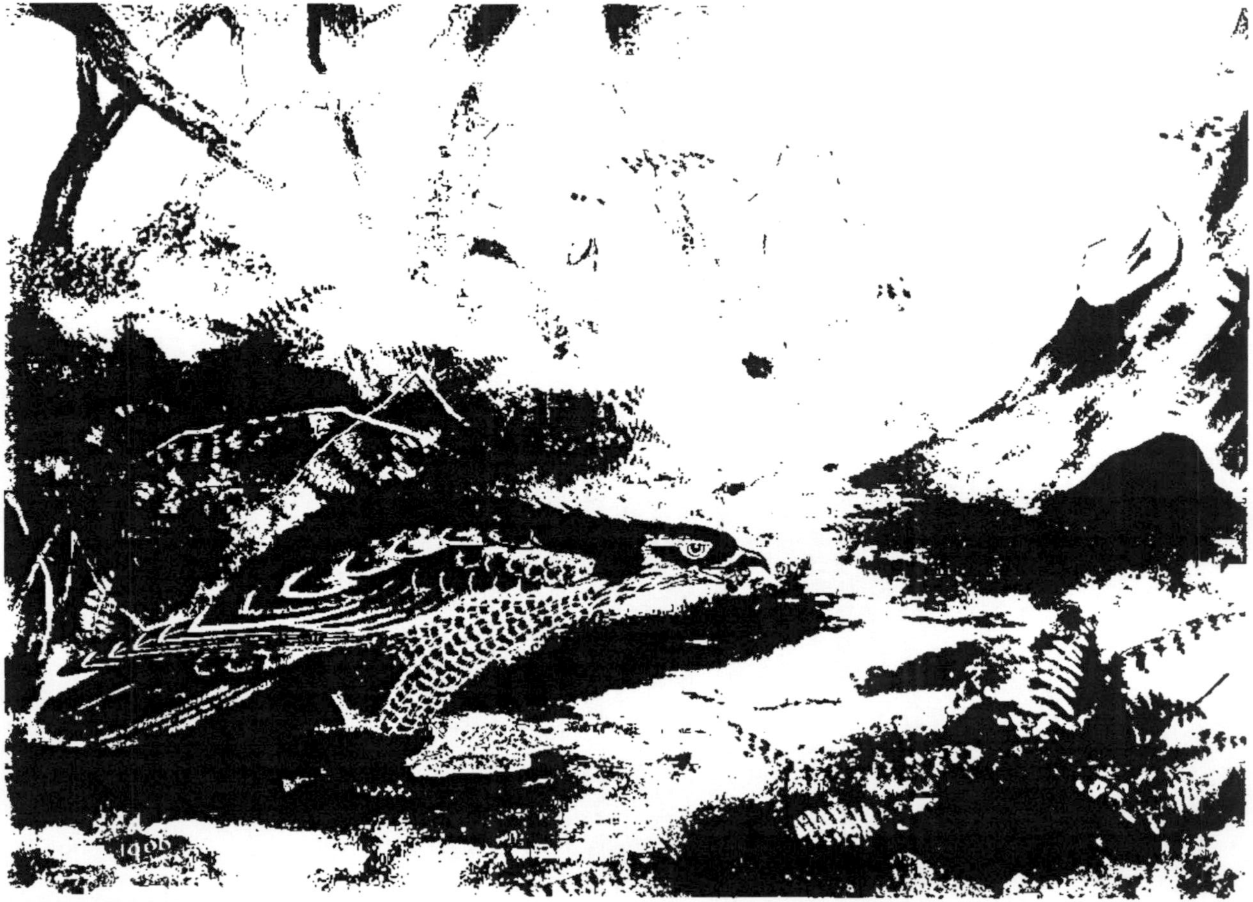

E. C. Arnold Del.] West Newman.

and bees themselves. A German observer has recorded that, in preying upon these insects, it seizes them crosswise in its beak and nips off the sting end of the body, which it allows to fall to the ground. . . . In attacking bees and wasps and their nests, it tears up the earth and comb very much as a hen scratches for its food. In this method of attack the bird is well provided by nature with defensive armour in the shape of its peculiarly thick plumage, especially about the head and throat. . . . It spends a good deal of its time on the ground, and when thus seen moves very like a Raven, with upstretched neck and ruffled neck-feathers."

The Corvidæ are, of course, common in such a locality, and hardly a season passes without eggs of the Magpie, Jay, and Carrion-Crow being brought to me for inspection; while, beside the Wood-Pigeon, the Turtle-Dove is to be found in most of the glades.

It was in these woods that I first made the acquaintance of the Tree-Pipit as a breeding species. It nests sparingly in the neighbourhood, the railway bank near Hellingly being, perhaps, its best known haunt. Distinguishable in the hand from the Meadow-Pipit by its curved hind claw, it is an easy bird to identify in spring time as it soars aloft and pours forth its song, which, though not beautiful, is sure to attract the attention of a passer-by. True, the Meadow-Pipit also sings while in the air, but he darts up and descends, somewhat after the manner of a Warbler. The Tree-Pipit, while singing, hovers more like a Kestrel; its wings look larger as it does so, and it hangs its legs and feet in such a way that they present the appearance of an inverted "T." The eggs, which, generally speaking, are redder than those of the Titlark, are very beautiful, when they happen to belong to the blotched variety, and the nest is not infrequently placed amongst the roots of a tree. By casual observers this Pipit is often confused with the Woodlark, which accounts for several reported occurrences of the latter bird. The Woodlark, however, is, as far as I can discover, quite a rarity in the district, and Mr. Bates tells me that he has very seldom had it brought to him. It should be distinguishable on the wing by its much shorter tail, and in the hand by the long and straight hind claw.

Far more beautiful and attractive than the Tree-Pipit, the Green Woodpecker, despite incessant persecution—I have often seen nooses hanging round its holes—still manages to maintain its numbers undiminished; and I have seldom made the journey to Polegate without seeing, or at all events hearing, one or more of these interesting birds. The fact is, the eggs are distinctly difficult to secure, and I have never known a boy actually get one. I hear every year of "new Woodpecker's holes certain to have eggs within a week, which it will be easy to get with putty and a wire," but a fortnight later you find, on enquiry, that something has gone wrong with the programme, and no eggs are forthcoming so far. I believe that this bird readily changes its nesting-site on suspicion ; and, as there are numbers of old holes available in these woods, it no doubt succeeds in baffling nesters in this way, for in July I almost always see youngsters along the outskirts of the copses. It is noticeable that most of the holes are on the sides of the trees farthest from the nearest path, and it is therefore quite easy to overlook them.

In 1905 one of these Woodpeckers must have had a *mauvais quart d'heure*, though it emerged triumphant in the end. A boy who knew little of ornithology saw a brightly coloured bird, which he judged to be a Parrot, fly into a hole in a tree. He left it unmolested at the time, but returned next day with a friend, a butterfly-net, and apparatus for the extraction of the eggs. The hole was out of reach of the ground, but he swarmed up and popped the net over it, while his accomplice hammered the tree with a thick stick. They kept the performance up until they were persuaded that Mrs. Parrot was not at home, a decision which was quickened by the sudden collapse of the climber's thigh-muscles. Down came the net, and up came the Woodpecker, which decamped with an exultant laugh and left the two conspirators feeling rather flat. However, there remained the eggs; they were still obtainable, if they could get at them. Number two now swarmed the trunk, and stuck to an uncomfortable position, until, at Nature's dictation, he too slid down. Such poking and scraping as he had managed to cram into his short excursion up aloft had produced some small pieces of white egg-shell and a little yolk, and this is the nearest approach to a Woodpecker's egg that I have ever known obtained near Polegate.

Some of the clearings in these woods are to my mind unusually attractive. One that contains a knoll carpeted in spring with bluebells, and producing a wonderful haze of blue in the distance, is a sight that no one could forget, while the track that leads to it contains the most effective of all woodland trees—a wild fruit-tree.

Other clearings, from which all the trees have been removed, have been overgrown with bracken, and thus afford a suitable breeding-ground for the Nightjar. There is little chance of finding the eggs amongst the thick cover, unless one happens to put up the bird, and the male is far more often flushed than the female. The latter, which can be recognized by the absence of the pure white spots on the primaries, seems to sit the closer, so close indeed that she sometimes falls a victim to a prowling stoat or rat;

at least such, I believe, to have been the history of a bird whose nest I once found, with one egg in it. I put the bird up, found the nest, and left it. But when, some days after, I was passing the same spot and looked in upon them, I was surprised to find the egg gone, while some tell-tale Nightjar feathers, scattered around what had been the nest, bore witness to a tragedy of the woods.

The Nightjar, when flushed, is said to fly usually to the nearest oak, and settle lengthwise on a branch; but one that I started pitched on a thin twig, where it sat crosswise, balancing itself somewhat awkwardly, a position which

A HAUNT OF BUTTERFLIES.

made its head look monstrous and out of all proportion to the size of its body. As is the case with the Stone-Curlew in districts where they are to be found, the natives always tell you that there are "dozens" about in the evening as soon as it gets dark; but the fact is that even a pair of Stone-Curlews or Nightjars gyrating about and screaming or jarring in the dusk will suggest the presence of quite half a dozen birds, and all statements as to numbers based on what has been seen after dark should always be accepted with reserve. I fancy two pairs of Nightjars are the utmost that any of these clearings could produce.

Woods of any sort are, in the main, sorry places for Warblers. I have often sought in vain for the Wood-Wren, spurred on at times by rumours that have reached me as to its presence.   Still, it is a bird one cannot overlook if it *is* present, and I am inclined to think that it is not.   So far, the Nightingale, which breeds freely, especially in the lanes leading to the woods, is the best member of the Sylviidæ that I have myself identified; but I was much excited once over the story of a shrewd and by no means over-confident observer, who stated that in a certain coppice he had seen two small Warblers of the Yellow family, like ordinary Willow-Wrens, but with strikingly light-coloured rumps, and a song that he did not recognize.   This information was given at a meeting of the College Natural History Society, but not by a boy, and I suggested that perhaps the strangers were Bonelli's Warblers, having in my mind's eye a vivid recollection of the lemon rump of a skin shown me by Mr. Gurney at the Norwich Museum some years before.   I went twice myself to see the birds, but I had not the finder with me, and it is doubtful whether I ever reached the spot.

These woods are no less satisfactory from the point of view of the entomologist.   The Purple Emperor has at all events been seen in them, and the Purple Hairstreak is common, while as for White Admirals, I have seen three captured at one sweep of the net!   The Marble White also occurs in small numbers; the large Pearl-bordered Fritillary is common. The Pearl-bordered Likeness was also common once, and two soulless hirelings from London are said to have captured three hundred in a week. Since then none have been seen.

CHAPTER XX.

WICKEN FEN.

Who has not at some time or other turned his thoughts towards the Fens? Who has not felt himself impelled to explore their historical and still interesting fastnesses, the refuge once of Hereward and the last of the Saxons; the refuge, in later days, of a different, but perhaps to the naturalist a not less attractive, race of beings—the Bittern, the Black Tern, the Black-tailed Godwit, and the Ruff?

It was not, however, with any hope of meeting with either of these rarities—which, if they then visited the place at all, did so only as stragglers on migration—that, on a glorious morning at the end of May, I set out from Cambridge, in company with three other kindred spirits, to see what bird-life could still be met with in this once famous district. I had often been sold before; often plodded gaily along to some place marked on the map as Fen "So-and-so," and as often returned worn out and disgusted, and inclined only to curse the march of civilization with all its hideous paraphernalia of dykes and causeways. I had reached my goal, and found it not, as I had fondly anticipated, a mass of sedge and water, but perhaps an ordinary green meadow sparsely sprinkled with a few decayed willows, or, worse still, an every-day sort of cornfield, differing little from its fellows, except that the soil was darker and heavier to walk upon.

On this occasion, however, there was no fear of disappointment. We were going to Wicken Fen, and had learnt from one who had visited the locality in person that we should at last see a genuine piece of fenland, undefiled by either railroad or ploughshare, and probably much the same as it had been a couple of centuries ago. We trained to Waterbeach, and intended to drive thence to the Fen. The route was easy to follow, as it led along the river all the way, but the only conveyance obtainable was a seedy-looking dogcart, drawn by a horse named, presumably in derision, "Wildfire"— a quadruped which looked as if, on a good road and pursued by wolves, it might perhaps have managed six miles an hour—and died after it. The road turned out to be a bad one; in fact, it soon degenerated into a species of quagmire, such as even in fenland is only dignified by the name of a drove. Through this we struggled steadily and slowly, the monotony of our journey being relieved on two occasions: first, when D——, who was quietly dozing on the back seat, slipped off and partially disappeared in one of the ruts; secondly, when, on turning a sharp corner, we found ourselves without warning in a farmyard, mixed up with a drove of cows. On arriving soon afterwards at an inn, which rejoiced in the quaint name of " Five Miles from Anywhere," we left our steed to recruit his flagging energies, and proceeded to the Fen on foot.

The first view was, it must be confessed, a trifle disappointing. Standing on higher ground, we could see right across it, a brown and monotonous but apparently insignificant expanse, which looked as if it could be traversed from end to end by fifteen minutes' hard walking. On the far side, however, a charming little hamlet, with churchyard and orchards, lay nestling in a fair-sized belt of trees, and on the outskirts of this village two or three windmills, thoroughly characteristic of the neighbourhood, were slowly revolving before the sluggish impetus of a summer's breeze.

After a short survey we once more started forward, and, though we soon began to find that distances in this flat country are deceptive, at last one field only, a rough uncultivated waste, remained to be negotiated. We had, when starting, discussed, though not seriously, the probability of meeting with that typical Fen butterfly, the Swallowtail; and scarcely had we passed through the gate when one darted by right under my nose. There was no mistaking, even on the wing, the pale yellow ground colour, with its dull black markings, and in a moment I was in hot pursuit, making up my net as I ran. The chase led straight across the field towards a high and impenetrable hedge on the opposite side, and, owing to the rugged nature of the ground, the odds seemed distinctly on the butterfly. It slackened off, however, as we neared the barrier, perhaps from fancied security, and I was enabled to get almost within striking distance. Five seconds more, and a well-directed sweep would have landed *Papilio* in the toils, when crash, smash, and I lay stretched out on the ground, a half-stunned heap of impotency, just able to get a glimpse of my quarry as it cleared the hedge in triumph. I had at the critical moment caught my foot in a rabbit-hole, introduced a spacious ventilator into the knee of my trousers, and for the time being utterly dislocated the net.

It was no use continuing the pursuit, which would have entailed a detour of half a mile, so we proceeded through a narrow belt of bushes to

the Fen itself. D—— entered one of the dykes ("lodes" the Fen people call them) to reach it, or, to be more accurate, a large portion of the dyke entered him, for the water, which seemed about three feet deep, rose to his mouth and over it, when he sank the same distance in the muddy slime at the bottom. The rest of us adopted milder methods, and crossed by a plank higher up, and then at length we had reached our destination.

WICKEN FEN.

Very different was the picture now before our eyes; the village seemed farther off than before, and, instead of a monotonous brown mass of reeds and osiers, we found numerous open spaces half under water, and studded with elegant wavy willow-bushes, clumps of bulrushes, and sweetly scented bundles of fresh-cut sedge. The surface of the Fen was varied; the whole was split up by narrow dykes or lodes of just such a width as to invite a jump, but with edges so rotten as to ensure a relapse. In parts the ground was dry and covered with long, waving grass; in others, you splashed through short sedge, where the water rose above the ankles at every step.

Where the pools were deeper the only method of progression was by a series of precarious leaps along the tussocks; and where the reeds were uncut it was almost useless to try and advance at all.

After a short rest we commenced our search. To our intense surprise Swallowtails swarmed on all sides, and we could have obtained literally any number of specimens; but they were quite alone in their glory—not a single other sort of butterfly was to be seen. The first nest found was that of a Snipe, which rose almost under our feet, and disclosed four eggs of a very dark colour. Several other Snipe were visible high up in the air, drumming and uttering their bleating note, mingled with the wild "pee weet" of the Lapwings, which were also breeding in some numbers on the Fen. Redshanks, too, are said to patronize it, but their eggs are very difficult to discover. The find of the day was a Kestrel's nest. The eggs, as is not unusual in this locality, were placed in a scantily lined hollow in the sedge, and we thought at first that they were Merlins'. We found, in addition, nests of the Turtle-Dove, Sedge-Warbler, Reed-Bunting, Bullfinch, and Redpoll, but were too early for those of the Reed-Warbler, birds which swarmed in every dyke.

While resting a few minutes from our exertions, our attention was suddenly attracted by a loud "chirring" noise, proceeding from a clump of sedge and willows two or three hundred yards away. We instantly recognized it as the note of the Grasshopper-Warbler, and, advancing cautiously, we obtained a distant view of the bird itself; but long and diligently as we searched, we failed to discover its nest, though a friend, who went rather later, found two, one in the side of a clump of sedge, the other almost on the ground. There is no mistaking the eggs, which are speckled so closely with tiny red spots that in many the ground colour at the larger end is quite obscured. The shade of red varies considerably, being in some cases light pink, in others almost the hue of cocoa. It was now growing dark, so we returned to the inn, and after a plain but hearty meal set "Wildfire" once more in motion, and arrived at Cambridge without further mishap.

Far different were the visits I used to make to the Fen in winter. It was such cold work driving, that we generally walked from Waterbeach along the river, there being just the chance of meeting with some Duck or Snipe on the way. At times Gulls frequented it, especially the Lesser Black-headed, and Grey Crows were almost always to be seen. It was the custom to put up the shooting, over a portion of the Fen, for auction at a local inn, the bidding being allowed to continue until a wax match burnt out. A friend of mine secured it one year, but as a Sniping ground the Fen was disappointing. I never saw as many Snipe in the winter as in the spring; six were the most we ever put up on a single day. As a rule you might walk miles without flushing a bird, but then the bird flushed might be a good one. It was thus that I once stumbled on a Bittern. In the hard winter of 1891 I had tramped ten miles without a shot, and was just on the point of giving it up, when there was a sudden commotion in a narrow belt of reeds beside the lode, and up blundered a monstrous bird. It was morally impossible to miss it, for it circled slowly round, and I was soon cautiously approaching it as it lay struggling on the ground. The shooting was a more simple matter than the getting it home. A stiff wind was blowing, and as I had lost my handkerchief earlier in the day it was impossible to tie it together, and I had to carry it as best I could, with its wings blowing about like the sails of a windmill, and glad indeed was I to reach Burwell, and stow it away in a grocer's box.

Other long winter tramps were not equally successful. You always got a shot just when you had ceased to expect it, and in this way I once missed six Duck that rose bang under my nose, to the unspeakable amusement of a friend, who had accompanied me for the sake of the grind. Still, the exhilarating sensations of the walk, enhanced as they were by the friendly attitude of the natives—from the old eel-spearer on the Fen to the newspaper boy at Burwell, who always provided us with the latest "special"—seldom failed to console us for our many failures, and leave us with the pleasantest recollections of the place.

In fact, if Wicken Fen can no longer produce the wonderful ornithological varieties of former days, there is, nevertheless, especially in the summer, still sufficient interest attaching to it to well repay the difficulties connected with a visit. The place, thanks to the public spirit of certain naturalists, is now said to be safe from the encroachments of the land reclaimer, and it is intended to be kept as a refuge for our rarer birds. Report says that even Bitterns have since bred on it, and reared their young unmolested; and, as the establishment of bird-sanctuaries is probably by far the best method of bird protection, it is to be hoped that the existing arrangements will long continue to remain in force.

CHAPTER XXI.

THE SHORE IN WINTER.

ONE cannot go into raptures over winter shore-tramping in the general. There are times, no doubt, when celestial is the only word that can describe the sport, golden moments when a sharp snack of frost has brought in the foreign Duck, and they are flying aimlessly about by day, backwards and forwards across the sea-wall, or occasionally dropping into some sheltered creek—"Duck coming in by the thousand," as the local phrase hath it. But how often do such welcome visitations coincide with the Christmas holidays? How often is such a picture descriptive of the actual facts? If you ask the village fowler for a definite date, seldom, if ever, can he give it you in the current year. Far more often it begins with, "When my father was a boy." No; a day's diurnal Duck-shooting on the open shore is a windfall to be revelled in as long as you can see the barrel of your gun, and then marked in one's diary as a red-lettered day.

The fact is, that in mild weather one has almost a better chance of getting a Goose than a Duck. The Grey-Lag and White-fronted in particular, are not infrequently to be seen coming off the sea in the morning, and making for the fresh marshes inside the wall, and if one has the luck to be behind it and in their line, there is every chance of securing a reasonable shot. If you miss it then, you may get a second opportunity towards evening, when they make their return journey seaward, or even earlier, if you can induce some cowherd to go and beat up his cattle on the marsh; but when they do move, after perhaps a three hours' wait on your part—for the average man will endure much for a shot at a Goose—even then your chance is a poor one. You may reckon on their coming against the wind, and more or less towards the line of the estuary, if there is one. But this leaves a wide margin outside the range of a twelve-bore, though a local, with his past experiences to help him, is not unlikely to hit off the exact line of their retreat.

But an ordinary winter's tramp across the saltings, how different it is to those blithe September days. Then, with only sand-shoes on our feet, we gaily worked our way along the channels, conscious that at each corner we might light on something good. There was the chance of a Red-breaster at all events, possibly even an American straggler driven out of its normal course. But all this is changed in the winter; those glorious possibilities are gone. The species of Waders to be met with are reduced to about half a dozen, and in their winter plumage we are quite contented to possess a single specimen of each. The Purple Sandpiper and the Godwit are, perhaps, the most attractive, the bluish tinge which then suffuses the latter's plumage making it, to my mind, more beautiful than the autumn bird. But the others—there is little to interest us in them. Moreover, they are all in flocks; you can see at a glance to what species they belong; the element of uncertainty which pertains to single birds is wanting; and as a rule the aforesaid flocks are so wild that, unless the weather is very hard, it is next to impossible to get near them. The difficulty is augmented by the fact that in winter one must wear boots, and boots, as opposed to sand-shoes, mean noise and much extra fatigue. So, unless the off-chance of a stray Wigeon appeals to the shooter with irresistible force, it is better in ordinary weather to abandon the saltings, and either proceed in a boat with decoys to the open sea after Duck and Divers, or concentrate one's efforts on the sand-hills and bushes, or the pools that run beside the rough sea-wall.

Here, if anywhere, we shall encounter a bird of prey. Buzzards, and even Eagles, condescend to pay the sand-hills a visit at times, and Harriers may more often be seen beating across their arid waste. There is, however, a reasonable chance of a Merlin. They are apt at this season to desert their moorland hunting-grounds, and descend to the region of the coast, where they pick up a ready sustenance by preying upon the smaller birds which frequent it. The first of these that attracts our attention is the Snow-Bunting. They may be seen in small parties along the sand-hills, dropping hither and thither with careless flight, their silver plumage gleaming bright against some dark-blue cloud. Many of them are more brown than white, but here and there may be seen some fine old cock—a snow-white beau amidst the mottled throng. They come regularly to the east coast in the winter, where they figure prominently in the daily menu of any Merlin that may happen to be about. Some days they are quite tame, hopping about contentedly almost at one's feet, but, if there is any wind blowing, it is often a difficult matter to secure a single bird.

Amidst the scrub at the edge of the saltings we are almost sure to meet with the Twite; it can be distinguished, while flying, from the Linnet by its slim form, more dusky plumage, and longer tail. At times, even in early January, I have secured a specimen with pink on the rump, but the

I

majority have not yet assumed this ornament of the breeding season. Mealy Redpolls are seen now and then amongst the flocks, though I have never come across one myself. Titlarks, of course, abound, and a bird that one would hardly expect to meet with, but which does crop up at times, is the Rock-Pipit; one recognizes it readily on the rock-bound coast, but here on the salt-marshes it is often overlooked; in fact, it was for long supposed to be a rare Norfolk bird. And hereby hangs a story. The dealer who first discovered it to be plentiful shot many, and, writing simultaneously to several well-known naturalists who collected county birds, asked each what he was prepared to give for a pair of Norfolk-killed Rock-Pipits. The savants each made an offer, based on Stevenson's estimate of the birds' rarity. Needless to say, these offers were accepted, and the purchasers returned in triumph with their spoils. The spirit of boastfulness which belongs to all collectors was not likely to make them conceal their acquisitions, but the gilt was off the gingerbread as soon as it became apparent that fortune had bestowed its favours on all alike. Hastily assuming that birds shot outside the county had been palmed off upon them, the whole body sought out the deceiver, and indignantly demanded an explanation of conduct so extraordinary.

"There is none," replied the unabashed salesman. "They are Norfolk birds, as I stated; the extraordinary thing is that you should have been willing to give such prices for them, when you might yourselves have shot dozens on the beach."

That evening a sadder and a wiser band, returning homewards from the sea-shore with lightened pockets if enlightened minds, was forced at length to confess from personal investigation that the Rock-Pipit was a common Norfolk bird.

If there happen to be any ricks in the neighbourhood, they will be well worth visiting in the winter, this being the most likely place to meet with a Cirl-Bunting, or that brightly coloured visitor from northern latitudes, the Bramble-Finch. But, after all, the prize to be sought for at this season of the year is the Shore-Lark. For long considered one of our rarest birds, it is now recognized that in most seasons it is fairly common on the sand dunes of the east coast; at times, indeed, flocks of thirty or upwards are to be seen there, but it is more often to be met with in small parties of half a dozen, sometimes mingling with the Sky-Larks, from which it may be distinguished readily by its note.

The Lapland-Bunting is another rarity that sometimes turns up amongst the bushes, but it is a hard bird to recognize, and is more often to be found on the fields. In the hand it can at once be distinguished by the length of the hind toe.

And now the sun is sinking, and the hour of the evening flight draws nigh. It is time to think of taking up one's station for the Duck. But, stay—what are those grey forms circling slowly round some unseen object on the shore? They are Hooded or Royston Crows, those ever restless *algæ inquisitores*, who are ceaselessly engaged in prying into the refuse above high-water mark, or poking their bills into the bushes to stir out any injured creatures that may, perchance, be harbouring beneath their shade. Their movements are always worth watching. This morning we came upon the mangled carcase of a Mallard, one that had escaped the search of the flight-shooters in the darkness, but was powerless to avoid the pitiless instinct of the Hoodie. So now, as we advance towards them, there is the momentary flash of a wing upon the shingle; and the reluctant way in which the Crows themselves retire before our approach confirms us in the belief that they were engaged in hunting down some ill-fated bird. We can see nothing, all the same, when we get there, even though we lie down flat on the shingle to get a surer view. After a short and fruitless search, we think it best to retire to the bushes, and, drawing out the field-glasses, keep a steady watch on the suspected place. Ah! there it *is* at last. A head is cautiously raised from the shingle, the form of a Duck follows it, and the owner makes off hurriedly for the sea. The moment we rise it disappears again, and the shore is to all appearances bare. But we have now got the line, and, advancing straight along it, soon perceive the form of a Wigeon drake, laid prone with neck outstretched in a shallow hollow midst the stones. It remains thus until we are within a few yards, hoping even now to escape, and then at last, its craft abandoned, it dashes frantically for the sea. It proves to be a foreign bird, smaller and compacter, but perhaps more beautiful, than the larger sort. It had been badly winged by some punter during last night's gunning in the estuary, and but for the astuteness of the Crows it might have lingered some days in agony without any chance of ultimate escape.

And now the Duck are beginning to bestir themselves. Standing beside a railway-carriage, we have a long crack at a Scaup beating in from the sea, and a little later, ensconced in the grass behind the sea-wall, we get shots, at uncertain intervals, at the flocks of Teal and Mallard that pass backward and forward across the marsh. Alas! all too fast, the precious half-hour runs out, and darkness sinks upon the dreary waste.

CHAPTER XXII.

THE MEADOWS IN WINTER.

THE water-meadows in winter! The prospect, it must be confessed, is not an inviting one, save, perhaps, to the ardent naturalist or the Snipe-shooter. It is too suggestive of damp feet, sore throats, colds, and possibly ague, to find favour with the average individual; and yet how attractive an insight into the life of many of our most interesting birds can then be picked up by anyone who is content to spend a single month in the diligent observation of ten or a dozen acres of ordinary Hampshire water-meadows.

It is a muggy December day, and, as you enter the first field, there rises in scattered and irregular detachments a flock of Fieldfares and Redwings, which are eagerly taking advantage of this short spell of mild weather to lay in provender against hard times to come. To-day they are as wild as Hawks, but when the snow and frost have lasted for a week and driven them to the bushes, even the Fieldfares will let you come close to them as they struggle with noisy chorus for the fast failing supply of berries to which they are now reduced for sustenance. The Redwings suffer most, as they are not really berry feeders; some approach the houses and frequent our gardens, but many may be picked up quite dead or helpless, and benumbed by cold and hunger.

We shall not see many of the larger birds to-day. The Plovers are feeding in the uplands, the Snipe—well, he may or may not be there; if he is, he will in all probability lie well, and be as fat as butter. It is the smaller birds that are in force: Skylarks and Titlarks swarm in every field, and take absolutely no notice of your approach, and the Kingfisher darts along the winding brook. Kingfishers appear in a marvellous way at this season, though many are never seen together. I met a man who had shot a dozen within a week from a single garden, and yet, walking in the meadows round, one would never have supposed that there were more than a couple in the neigh-bourhood. Perhaps, however, as is the case with Falcons, single pairs reserve a district for themselves, and it is by new arrivals that the places of the slain birds are, in a suitable neighbourhood, so regularly filled.

Next, one's attention is attracted by the incessant and ubiquitous chirping of a family party of Long-tailed Tits, as, tempted forth by the mild atmosphere and the sunshine, ·they flit along the hedges beside the streams on their way to some favourite copse or fir-wood. Here they are always to be found when the weather becomes more severe. A rarer and more welcome sight would be a small flock of Siskins, and these, if seen at all, will be hanging like Tits in every conceivable attitude from the boughs of an alder. I once met a single Siskin not far from St. Cross, and made an effort to get it with a walking-stick gun, but the barrel was so corroded with rust that the shot positively failed to get through it, and the bird escaped. Lesser Redpolls often accompany the Siskins, and resemble them much in habits and general appearance; their song is, however, weak and monotonous, and they have few qualities to recommend them beyond their cheerfulness. When the sun is behind them, and you cannot see the colours, Siskins and·Redpolls may always be distinguished from Tits by their forked tails, which are noticeable even at the top of fair-sized trees.

Little more will be seen to-day, unless it be the fleeting form of a Hawfinch, or perhaps a Moorhen as she disappears into a clump of reeds, or the saucy little Dabchick, which seems to positively revel in the icy waters.

And now the scurrying clouds and the biting blast of the north-easter foretell the approaching storm, and you wake on the morrow to find the ground covered with a sheet of snow. Let us wait a few days until the change has had time to tell upon the birds, and then sally forth once more. The first to attract us are the Peewits; they are present in numbers, driven down from the upland fields to the marshy dips, where the water has thawed the snow, and left bare a scanty feeding-ground. Some are foraging singly, and, wary as ever, seldom allow a near approach; but others are flying backwards and forwards, as if uncertain whether it would not be better policy, after all, to migrate at once to the unfrozen oozes of the sea-shore. These latter afford many a shot to the patient gunner who lurks hidden in the centre hedge. Sometimes, too, a small party of Golden Plover appears upon the scene, following the main river on its way to the sea. They may be recognized by their brownish appearance, peaked wings, swift flight, and their way of keeping the head close to the shoulders. One rarely sees much of them, for, unlike the Peewit, they go ·steadily on in one direction, never staying long in any particular meadow.

But what is this curious dark little creature that has just fluttered up almost from beneath our feet—all legs and body it seems, with tiny wings that can barely support its weight ?   It is a Water-Rail, a bird not particularly rare, but seldom seen except in hard weather, owing to its skulking habits ; and even now, though you may flush it once by accident, it is not often that it can be induced to rise again and give you a second view.

On such a day as this, one may often see the Heron flapping himself along, high up and well out of gunshot, and, if the surrounding district is wild and fortune unusually propitious, it is just the time for meeting with that interesting rarity, the Common Bittern.   No home-bred bird is he in these days, but some travel-wearied migrant from the Continent, whose probable fate on our hospitable shores will be a dose of lead, and hereafter a distinguished position in the museum of some heaven-favoured collector.

Perhaps the greatest rarity I ever met with myself in the winter was a Great Grey Shrike.   The bird was in a hedge not far from the triangular meadow at Twyford, but it was very wild, and quite unapproachable, though I managed to get close enough to be certain of the species.   Within a few yards of the same spot I came upon a Greater Spotted Woodpecker in the following year.   It was examining a decayed branch which had fallen from one of the lofty elms, and, being armed at the time with a small walking-stick gun, I instituted an elaborate stalk.   By making a long circuit and then crawling some distance on my knees, I reached the far side of the elm-tree unobserved.   I could hear the bird tapping within a few feet of me, and it was a case of who would see the other first, when I put my head round the corner.   Slowly and cautiously I peered round, with gun up and finger on the trigger, but, as bad luck would have it, his head only was exposed, and, quickly as I fired, the bird was quicker, and off he flew from amidst a cloud of dust and bark.   I used to see him regularly afterwards for some days, climbing up the willow-trees, but never again did I get near enough for a shot.

The Green Woodpecker and the Nuthatch are also to be met with at times amidst the decaying timber.   The former is only a casual visitor from Twyford Park, but the Nuthatch can often be discovered, sometimes close up to the city ; in fact, I have seen one in the Close.

Such are the birds that frequent the meadows in the morning, and, besides these, both Jacks and Common Snipe are to be met with at all times, while Kestrels, which have left the cultivated fields, can be seen here and there hovering high up throughout the day.

And now for a last visit in the evening ; and this will well repay anyone who undertakes it, provided, of course, that he has a good warm coat on, and watertight boots.   It will be rather ticklish work picking one's way out of

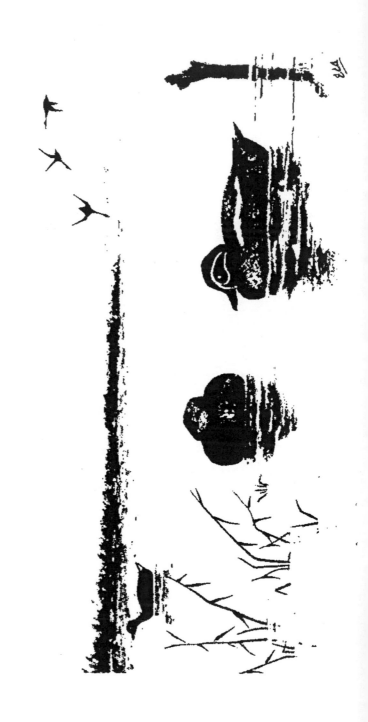

these semi-frozen swamps when the sun has set, but at present you are comfortably located on a paling concealed by the hedge, and have settled yourself down for a quiet and interesting half-hour. There is a certain weird charm about a winter's sunset in the water-meadows, which harmonizes well with the muffled shriek of the Peewits as they loom big in the darkness previous to taking up a station for the night. A white shadow flits noise-lessly from behind, and is lost to sight in a moment; it is the Barn-Owl, quartering the fields in his nightly search for mice; and now a Kestrel slowly wings its way past your ambush to its evening resting-place. It is time to look out for the Duck, and here they come, travelling high up in the air, from some preserved pond three miles off, perhaps, where they have spent the day in safety. As they near the meadows, they descend gradually and noiselessly, no longer with the quick flaps that have carried them along so far, but with a silent ghostly motion they glide hither and thither in the gloom, an occasional "quack" and sharp splash showing that one has at last found a feeding-place to his liking.

But we must now think of retiring; and well for us if we have taken note of the ground by day and can strike the solid places at the first attempt; otherwise our expedition is likely to have an uncomfortable termination. Crossing rickety ice-bound planks is a trying ordeal at any time, but the chances of a catastrophe are indefinitely augmented when the passage has to be negotiated with only the uncertain assistance of the moon.

CHAPTER XXIII.

LEADENHALL MARKET.

It is a common saying that visitors can find little to do in London during the morning. The man of business finds in his work occupation sufficient, perhaps more than sufficient, to satisfy his utmost requirements; but the case is different with the country cousin who has come up to London to see the sights. He will find few places of amusement open before lunch, and after having duly digested the standing dishes provided by the Zoo, National Gallery, St. Paul's, and Westminster, he will not improbably towards the end of his visit find the mornings hanging heavily on his hands. Under such circumstances, if he happen to be the possessor of any ornithological instincts whatever, he may well do worse than pay a visit to Leadenhall Market.

One would not, it is true, instinctively regard the centre of London as a suitable locality for a natural-history ramble; but the aforesaid market is in many respects unique, and it is quite possible that a man may see there more varieties of large birds in half an hour than he would meet with during a twelvemonth spent in the country. Few members of the Duck tribe have not at some time or other adorned this great emporium of the Anatidæ, and during a casual visit at the beginning of February I counted no fewer than twenty-five species, all of more or less interesting birds. Passing through the main archway, one comes at once to the largest shops—some poulterers, some fishmongers, some butchers, their wares often strangely intermingled as the carcasses are hastily unpacked. Straight before us looms the form of a Swan, "wild" so-called, but in reality a tame bird driven by the frost to the sea-shore, and there stalked and butchered by some local Nimrod. Presumably all the natives fought shy of it, and it has found its way to Leadenhall, and now, suspended by a hook through its beak, it awaits the arrival of some venturesome purchaser—someone confident in his digestive organs, and the possession of adamantine teeth.

We pass on to the next stall, and that long symmetrical line of Wigeon. What a scene it suggests!—the joyous company feeding or preening their feathers on the mudflats, the gliding punt, the heavy boom of the punt-gun, the sharp reports of the cripple-stoppers, and the triumphant return to the shore.

Or this half-emptied box of Dunlins. Can we not picture the "'long-shore" gunner as he steals upon the unsuspecting flock, and ruthlessly rakes them while still standing on the muds, and all to provide one of the most disappointing dishes that ever man was invited to partake of, for no one ever has been, or ever will be, found to say that he likes Dunlin? Hard by, an epicure is examining some Golden Plover, carefully scrutinizing the feet, lest the presence of a hind toe betray the fact that they are really "Grey"; and further on, again, some collector is haggling over the price of a Golden-Eye, the salesman expatiating on the perfect condition of the bird, while the would-be purchaser insists that it is badly shot in the neck and will never make a respectable specimen.

Many naturalists regularly visit the market in search of rarities, and many are the rare birds which have been secured in this way. Varieties of the genus Grebe and Crake, and, in the spring time, Ruffs from Holland, are prizes which one may always hope to pick up; and though this cannot be considered the most sporting method of increasing one's collection, yet there is nevertheless a certain fascination in spying out the birds; and when rheumatism and old age have conspired to stop our visits to the saltings, Leadenhall presents itself as a substitute, and, for want of a better, is welcomed by many, if only because it serves as a connecting-link with the never-to-be-forgotten triumphs of the past.

Here we may renew acquaintance with the Pintail, one of the most elegant of all the Ducks. They are to be seen sandwiched in between Pochards, Teal, Wigeon, and Mallards, while here and there is suspended an odd specimen of the Tufted Duck, or perhaps a Red-throated Diver, caught napping in some seaside estuary, and despatched to London in a mixed consignment of Thrushes, shore-birds, and wild-fowl. In fact, as is the case with shore-shooting, the uncertainty as to what may turn up next is one of the chief elements that lend interest to a stroll round the market. The salesmen are quick to divine the motives of the purchaser, and if they think he is buying the bird to stuff, the price will vary in accordance with a rough estimate as to the limits of their victim's gullibility.

Turning out of the main thoroughfare into the labyrinth of dark and narrow passages on the right, we come to that section of Leadenhall which is given up to the vendors of live-stock. In one cage two rabbits are quietly munching their cabbage, wholly oblivious of the fact that their next-door neighbour, a fox-terrier, with ruff erect, is straining every nerve to get at them. Jays, Ducks, cats, and squirrels fill up the rest of the row, and on the shelf above two Curlews (saddest sight of all), begrimed with dirt and unable to raise a tail between them, are mournfully stalking round their prison, ever and anon darting their long beaks with spasmodic and painful jerks between the bars— a weird uncanny couple, hardly to be recognized as relations of the handsome birds that we have watched so often amidst the natural surroundings of the shore.

Beside these sits a Merlin, so blackened by smoke that he might easily pass as a melanism, brooding perhaps, in doleful silence, over the days when he, too, skimmed in rapturous freedom across the marshes, or chased the flying Titlark on the moor.

It is a melancholy spectacle to linger over, and we leave them with the hope that they may at least find their way to some spacious aviary, or the still less irksome confinement of a lawn.

Many other creatures, both furred and feathered, might be added to the above-mentioned list, for Leadenhall is in some respects a second edition of the old Seven Dials; but the pitiful vision of those unfortunate Curlews has done much to allay our curiosity, and we have lost the desire for further investigation of their cells.

CHAPTER XXIV.

LOST OPPORTUNITIES.

"Whatever's hit is history, and what is missed is mystery." This, I believe, is a recognized axiom amongst bird collectors; and I propose to write a few words about some of those mysterious creatures which have succeeded in baffling the efforts of my well-intentioned, but misdirected, discharge.

Fanciful as it may seem to many, there is a certain morbid pleasure to be derived from speculating and theorizing on the subject of the birds that one has missed. There are people, of course, who never do miss. Who has not seen the whites of some boatman's eyes, so piously exposed in pity, after some quite excusable miss?

"Well, it was sixty yards off if it was a dozen, and on the right-hand side of the boat," you say by way of exculpation.

"Aye, aye, sir; but I counts a bird dead at eighty, if I once claps eyes on him; you ought to have got him, and no mistake."

"Then take the gun and get one yourself," is your angry rejoinder, as another Wader comes twisting into range.

Bang! Bang! No result so far as you can see, but your boatman has better eyesight. "Peppered her nicely just in front of the tail," he explains quite cheerfully; "she won't go far, I warrant; look how she's heeling over even now!"

You see no signs of any heeling over, nor, in fact, of anything unusual in the bird's flight, but you feel also that a valued reputation is at stake, and having had your own self-esteem restored to you by what was in reality a palpable miss, you gracefully accept the man's version, and agree with him in everything save the somewhat half-hearted proposal to "weigh anchor and go after her." For myself, I confess without any false shame that I miss far more often than I hit. I regard myself as a moderate shot when on the spot; if off it—i.e., if handicapped by a liver or any extraneous incubus, such as a supercilious gamekeeper or a boatman—most people would describe me as bad outright.

True, I did on one red-lettered day—23rd December, 1899—kill nine Snipe with eleven cartridges, one bird only escaping me, for one fell to my second barrel. But that this really happened scarcely any, save the few who saw them in the flesh, have ever believed; fewer still have ever satisfactorily explained the phenomenon, and amongst these latter was certainly not my spaniel "Shot," for by the time the ninth bird fell he seemed quite scared, and evidently thought there was something uncanny about so unorthodox an exhibition on my part.

From this piece of undisguised bragging, pardonable, perhaps, in one who so rarely does anything worth bragging about, I return to the chastening contemplation of the far more numerous birds that I have missed. Of course one may easily be mistaken in the matter of supposed misses. Had I missed a bird which I shot in 1903 on the Norfolk sand-hills, I should always have imagined that I had let go a Killdeer Plover. This bird rose from the grass, and flew straight away from me. By its shape I judged it to be a Plover, and as it had a bright red rump I thought it must be a Killdeer, and brought it down. What was my disgust, when I got there, to find that it was an immature Grey Plover, previously wounded, and with its rump soaked with blood.

After all, the getting or missing of rarities is to a great extent a matter of luck, so much depends on when and where they turn up. I shudder now to think how near I was to losing my Pectoral Sandpiper at Aldeburgh. I certainly do not owe its acquisition to my marksmanship, about which, as regards that particular occasion, the less said the better. The bird now adorns my collection because it happened to have a penchant for a special spot, and because it was also—alas for it!—a bird of unusual persistency. What I suspect I shall always regard as the miss of my life was the missing of a Sociable Plover on the Norfolk coast in September, 1903. This bird, though it has failed to secure—perhaps I should say successfully eluded—a place in history, can, I think, in the realms of mystery, take precedence over all other aspirants to renown.

Its pursuit was in this wise: My brother started it on a circular sandy plain; wind S.S.E., weather fine. From the start it judged the range of a twelve-bore to a nicety, and for two hours he escorted it about the estuary, engaging in firing exercise whenever he got inside one hundred yards, which was not very often. During this time the bird occasionally soared aloft, and then returned to the plain for a run. Its appearance was so unusual that the mussel-seekers, a race of beings whose stolidity I have never before known to be upset, left their work and spontaneously joined in the pursuit, making a futile effort to drive it over the gun. The bird then made for the sea-shore proper, and alighted on a shingle bank. In following it thither my brother met me, and I also took up the pursuit. From his account I did not think there was much chance of getting within range. This, however, we nearly achieved, and had I not been foolish enough to stop and turn my glasses on to it, I shall always think we should just have got a reasonable shot. As it was, the bird rose directly we resumed our advance, and I only got in a long hurried shot with the left barrel; and that was the last that I personally saw of the Sociable. It was facing me, as I looked through the glasses, with its cheek turned, and it had a Plover's head, with a conspicuous light stripe above the eye; it might have been from this view a huge immature Dotterel. On the wing it appeared somewhere about the size of a Lapwing, with very black and white wings.

On the following day my brother re-established communications with the stranger on the sands; it ran straight for the highest sand-hill, and scuttled up to the top. Needless to say, he got no shot there; it again did some soaring. Seeing that the bird had so well gauged the range of a twelve-bore, we hoped to outwit it on the next day by taking out a double-barrel eight, but, though we dragged this weighty piece of ordnance about for the best part of fifteen miles, we never got a glimpse of the Sociable, which for us was henceforth a lost bird. As we afterwards discovered, other shooters had seen our bird, and had been equally struck with it. One couple, so they said, put it out of a furze-bush on a sheep-walk, but from what I know of the said sheepwalk I suspect it was only amongst some scattered furze-bushes, not in one. I have seen Golden Plover amongst them at other times. The one had judged it to be a Little Bustard, which was reasonable; the other proclaimed it a Bittern, which was absurd. What Bittern would stroll about on an open sandy plain, or disport itself on shingle, in broad daylight? I can vouch for its not being a Thick-knee, a bird I know well; so if it wasn't a Sociable, what was it? Someone suggested a Courser, but I saw it well enough to be sure that there was no black streak near the eye, and the only other tenable suggestion was an Isabelline Lapwing. If so, it had made away with its crest, and was apparently ostracized by its own genus, for there were no other Lapwings about.

So much for the Sociable Plover. A few days later, in the same locality, I added another good bird to my list of derelict rarities. This was a Harrier, probably a female Montagu. I was enjoying a frugal lunch with a friend in a moist depression on the marsh, when far off, but straight in front of us, I spied the long peaked wings and the short neck of a large raptorial bird. I lay perfectly still until its facial disc was apparent, well within range, and passing me about forty yards off on the left side. Then I whipped up my gun, took a steady aim, and pulled the trigger. Soul of a Crow! It was half-cocked. I had forgotten that we were having lunch, and rapidly as I cocked the left barrel and got it into action, the effort was too late, the chance was gone; the Harrier had left us *en route* for Africa, or maybe the South Pole, to judge by the style of her departure. As for my companion, Flattery herself would find it difficult to eulogise his share in the catastrophe; he sat through it all with both barrels at full-cock, and forgot to fire either of them!

Rarity number three owed his or her escape to my innate humanity, collector though I am. It was September, and I was dreamily strolling along a reed-fringed dyke on my way to take up a station for the evening flight. Out popped a Reed-Warbler; at least, was it a Reed-Warbler? Yes, I somewhat lazily decided it was, though with rather a striking head. Again it appeared, fluttering up to the top of a reed, and again that very white cheek caught my eye. Still I did not fire; a Reed-Warbler is too nice a bird to kill on speculation, and I had not come to take it very seriously yet; I did not even cock my gun. And now we were approaching a dense reed-bed at the end of the dyke, and my little friend, keeping near the water, did not emerge again until he reached the very last of the open reeds. Then he fluttered up, and as he did so the light of the setting sun caught him fair. Could I believe my eyes? There were dark bars across the tail. For a moment I did not grasp their full significance, and then, like a flash, there came upon me Mr. Frohawk's picture in 'British Birds.' The attitude had happened to be the same; I was convinced that I had seen a Savi. By the time I had realized all this the bird was in the reed-bed, and I was never able to dislodge it. Sceptics, of course, will smile. I should in their place, but I shall always believe, nevertheless, that I have been privileged to behold a specimen of this long-lost denizen of our fens.

With the last-mentioned bird I close my record of "lost opportunities." Other collectors must have had many similar experiences, but most prefer to bury them in oblivion. They don't enjoy laughing at themselves, and still less do they enjoy being laughed at by others; and so, for the most part, they seek their consolation in a good dinner, and endeavour to persuade themselves that the bird palpably was not that which they most certainly thought it was when they were proceeding to fire at it, and had not yet missed.

But, after all, most of us can treat misses with some sort of equa-

nimity. "All in the day's job," we say. "Besides, who knows? I may
see it again to-morrow." But what if in the evening there appears upon
the scene that miserable kill-joy, the man who didn't miss; who drags
forth from the recesses of his game-bag, and expects you to admire, and,
worse still, congratulate him on having slaughtered, the bird that you had
ear-marked as your own? Well, I make no secret of the fact that it is
an occasion for displaying Christian charity to which I personally have
never yet risen. Were I to express my real feelings in polite English, I
should say: "Sir, if I were absolutely certain that, but for your skill as
a marksman, the bird in question would now be well on its way to France,
I should be able to congratulate you with sincerity; but this I feel is a
very big 'if.' Confound you, sir, why didn't you miss it, too?"

CHAPTER XXV.

UNUSUAL SHOTS.

THE reader who, on seeing this title, has resigned himself to some tall stories on the subject of long-distance shots can rest assured that he will escape them. I, too, have heard the yarn of the sportsman who, firing at a Partridge across a river, killed also a trout which rose at that moment, and then, in amazement at his exploit, staggered backwards and sat down upon a hare! I have also heard of a veteran shooter's six hundred odd Starlings killed at a single discharge, and who am I that I should seek to measure swords with these leviathans? A collector, moreover, has a soul above such details as the number of yards at which he bagged his specimen; it is enough for him that he has got, or missed, his bird.

Still, I have seen strange shots made with guns in my time; yes, and with other implements than guns, for the first unusual shot that I remember was made, not with a gun, but with a catapult, and it was as unpleasant as it was unusual. I had started a theory that it would be possible to shoot more accurately—no minor consideration with a catapult—if we held the fork much more forward instead of straight up. Full of zeal for my invention, and anxious to prove its excellence, I rushed into the garden to test my theory on the first Sparrow that came my way. I returned with equal precipitation, bawling for boracic-lint and a bandage. The shot in its eagerness to reach the victim had taken a short cut through the top of my thumb, and left a long smooth furrow behind it.

Our catapults had not long yielded to the superior destructive power of a ·410 collector's gun, when, one soft summer's evening, just as it was turning dusk, I espied from my bedroom window the substantial form of a Brown Owl, seated placidly on one of the chimneys of a neighbour's house in Winchester. A raptorial bird just across the road, and we the possessors of a genuine gun! Flesh and blood could not have resisted. Out came the weapon; for a moment it rested on the window-bar, and then a roar as of thunder echoed through every cranny of the Cathedral Close. Out rushed a footman from one house, a cook and two housemaids from the next, and up charged the rest of our family expecting to find one corpse at least on the premises, if not two.

They found us looking rather blankly out of the window. That confounded Owl! it had just done the one thing that neither of us had anticipated. We had expected it to fall off the chimney-pot, down the roof, and into the lane below, and the programme was to let it lie there until it got a bit darker and the excitement had cooled down. Not a bit of it; the moment it was hit, it threw up its wings, waltzed once madly round the chimney-pot, and then to our unspeakable confusion disappeared down the inside. It was with no small relief that we learnt the Canon was away, and not returning till the morrow. There were only the servants to be dealt with; so we set off, rang the bell, and stating that "we had reason to believe" there was an Owl in one of their chimneys, which might give trouble during the night, we considerately offered to relieve them of so uncanny a visitor. No questions were asked as to the grounds for this belief; the offer was accepted with alacrity, and we were soon escorted to the attic to which the chimney was supposed to belong. I reconnoitred it with caution. The Owl was there, very much there, so was his beak and so were his claws. Moreover, he occupied a commanding position on a narrow ledge about a foot up. It was a situation we had not foreseen, and it was complicated by the absurd behaviour of the servants. They had had time to put two and two together, and, having grasped that the Owl was wounded and therefore doubtless vicious, they clamoured wildly for its expulsion. No one, however, showed any symptoms of a desire to close with the creature, and matters seemed verging towards a deadlock, when my brother suggested getting a butterfly net. The net was brought, and I stole towards the chimney, made a dab and missed, the result being that the Owl fluttered up on to a higher ledge.

Here was a poser, indeed; in order to make another attempt it was necessary to put one's head right into the chimney, and as the possibility of having an eye extracted, in the endeavour to extract the Owl, evidently found favour with no one, it was decided to leave him there for the night. One servant did, it is true, suggest that the chimneys were connected, and "what was there to prevent his getting into theirs?" I boldly asserted that he was too much damaged to do this, and though the speed with which I had retired from the recent tussle might well have thrown a doubt upon the statement, the discrepancy escaped notice, the door was locked, and we retired to think out a new plan of campaign for the morrow. No one devised anything more brilliant than putting a longer stick in the

K

butterfly net, and without any great confidence in our resources we returned in the early morning to the attack. It proved an easier business than we had dared to hope. The Owl had dropped down to the lower ledge, and seemed, poor creature, very groggy, but though I got the net over him with comparative ease, he fought like a demon when once in the toils, and there was much work for Aesculapius before he was finally subdued.

It is not often that a premonition that a gun is likely to burst is regarded by its owner as a valid reason for trying to sell it second-hand to an unsuspecting friend, but it has been so once, at all events. The friend in question expressed a desire to try it first, and was invited by the owner to accompany him to a neighbouring marsh. At the first shot the gun kicked violently; so with the second; after the third the prospective purchaser found himself on his back in the mud seeing stars. The owner, not one whit abashed, strolled up to him. "Well, I'm blessed if I didn't think she was going to bust soon," was his apt comment on the event.

How many people, I wonder, know the exact range of a gun? If I don't myself I ought to, for I learnt it by experience the very first day I ever went shore-shooting. I arranged with another novice that we should take it in turns to sit in a stranded boat and shoot, while the other drove. I drove first, and with great success steered a small flock of Dunlin straight for the boat. My friend fired while they were still straight, and the only thing hit was myself. I was fairly peppered, though fortunately in no vital spot. But after all there was somewhere about a hundred yards between us, and the experience of the boatman who went out with a keen but short-sighted collector must have been far more terrifying than my own.

He worked his man up to such a pitch of excitement by his successful whistling and his multitudinous directions that the sportsman, feeling, I suppose, that there was a bird to be shot somewhere, though he could not see it, finally let drive at some imaginary Wader underneath the rower's arm—a shot which stopped not the bird but the boat, for it blew a hole in the bows and sank her!

It is marvellous that more accidents do not happen amongst shore-shooters when one considers the treacherous walking and the general recklessness that supervenes on all sides if a Duck does happen to put in an appearance during the day. It seems a recognized case of *sauve qui peut*, so far as onlookers are concerned. Not that Ducks are always unapproachable on salt water. One of the softest shots I ever saw was made at a September Wigeon in an estuary. I was rowing barely clear of the houses, and just coming up to the flock of village Ducks that one always met at that particular corner.

"Mind where you're going, or you'll brain one of these Ducks," said the shooter in the bows as we got amongst them.

"You mind your own business and shoot that brown one if he rises," was my answer, as I glanced over my shoulder and half saw a rather trim-looking bird amongst the flock. The words were hardly out of my mouth, when up it got not five yards off the boat. Streeten's gun missed fire, and Young had his back turned, but the Wigeon was considerate and settled hard by in the marsh. Out sprang two eager schoolboys and went after it; and their combined efforts worried it into a premature grave in the estuary. On the same day my brother aimed at a Skua, and killed the Tern it was chasing—one of the flattest shots I have ever seen made.

During a September migration, a small Warbler attracted my attention on the mud at the side of a tidal drain. Not recognizing it, I fired and apparently killed it, as it did not fly away; but on reaching the spot I found only one or two breast-feathers, round which the mud was churned up. I thought at first I had buried it, but that was not so, and to this day I am utterly mystified as to what really happened to that bird.

I was once with a friend who fired from above at a bird in a large drain. The bird decamped unharmed, and he then murmured rather feelingly that there were no shot-marks in the mud. I, of course, suggested that he had missed the drain as well as the bird, but, if so, it was a record shot of its kind, and we charitably assumed afterwards that he had somehow got hold of a blank cartridge, though in that case it was singular that he should have happened to use it when he had mud for a background.

Do birds ever die or become disabled from pure fright when they are fired at? More than once I have seen birds supposed to be shot which showed no signs of a wound, either then or when being stuffed. Our first Bluethroat was a case in point. My brother, R. B., fired at it on some shingle. The bird then ran towards him, and being too near to shoot again, and fancying it was injured, he made at it and captured it with his hand. I could never find the slightest trace of an injury when I came to set it up.

Walking-stick guns are provocative of more gusty language than any other sporting implement I have ever encountered, golf clubs not excluded, but I made a most memorable shot with one all the same. It was near Cambridge that I was walking along a hedge with a friend, out of which repeatedly popped a Hedge-Sparrow. He suggested after a time that I should have a shot at it on the wing; my weapon was the smallest-sized walking-stick with which I had never even tried to kill on the wing before. I refused several times, but at the end of the hedge was another at right angles to it, and connected by a five-barred gate. As we approached I remarked: "Well then, I'll pot it through the bars of that gate as it flies across." I fired as it did so, and when we got up there lay the bird!

I bought soon afterwards a twenty-bore walking-stick gun, second-hand, and an awesome weapon it proved to be. You never knew whether it was or wasn't going off, and the man who sold it to me very untruthfully asserted that it could be used with or without its detachable stock. I tried it the first day at Aldeburgh without the stock, taking a sitting shot at what I hoped was a Dusky Redshank. I held it at half the length of my arm, and the thing came back like a piston, catching me just below my nose and knocking me more or less silly. Though conscious that I was badly hurt, the wound was somewhat numbed for the moment, and as the Redshank circled round and pitched on nearly the same spot, I was idiot enough to fire again, though this time I did so with my arm at full stretch. Again the gun sprang back, and caught me this time on the forehead, though without cutting it. I was now becoming painfully aware of the extent of my first injury, and made off home as fast as I could. I found a gaping cut all along the top of my moustache, and after it had been sewn up I went for a fortnight in mortal dread of a sneeze, and without even the acquisition of the Dusky to console me. I then returned the gun at a reduced price to the vendor, and fancy he is likely to do a good business with it before it eventually bursts, for I suspect the term "second-hand" was a bit of a euphemism even when I bought it.

Once in Norfolk I fully believed that I was the witness of an actual death. A man was shooting from a boat with very little regard for those outside it, as I had already become aware. Another shooter was waiting in an adjacent creek, and some shore birds came sailing over the sand. The man in the boat followed them shamelessly towards the shore tramper and fired. There was an awful shriek, and the man rolled over on his back, waving his leg frantically to the accompaniment of the most blood-curdling yells. We all rushed to the spot, the shooter ghastly to behold; but there was no tragedy in it after all. The fellow was shamming to give the other man a lesson, and that he most certainly did.

For the benefit of those who missed it, I cannot refrain from concluding with a story that was published in the 'Globe.' The scene was a Highland hotel, the hero a distinguished colonel returned from a day's shooting along the shore.

"Any sport to-day, colonel?" asked a friend, as they were sitting down to dinner.

"Not much, very bad in fact," replied the warrior. "Still, I met a seal in the estuary on my way back and had three shots at it, a miss each time."

Shortly afterwards there entered another visitor with a bandage round his head, and his hand in a sling.

"Hallo, had an accident?" inquired the colonel.

"Accident!" replied the other with a vindictive snort; "attempted murder I call it. I was having a quiet bathe in the estuary, when up came some lunatic of a shooter and fired at me three times."

The colonel hurriedly turned the conversation to the Japanese War.

CHAPTER XXVI.

NOTES ON BIRD PRESERVING.

MANY are the treatises that have been written on bird-stuffing, many the strange representations of Nature that obedience to their instructions has produced, and many the internal shudders that have been experienced by those whom the artist has invited to admire them.

I do not intend, therefore, to describe the whole process in detail. Full directions can be bought anywhere for a shilling, and any one of these hand-books will answer its purpose perfectly well. Myself, as one who never had a lesson on the subject, and owes most of his skill, such as it is, to the bitter teaching of experience, I only propose to jot down a few hints and suggestions which may perhaps save some youthful collector from the feeling of unspeakable vexation with which I have often gazed upon the remnants of those rarer birds which I was unfortunate enough to capture, and subsequently mangle, in the earlier days of my collection.

To one who regards a stuffed bird from an æsthetic rather than a scientific point of view, few sights are more intensely maddening than that of a rare bird badly stuffed. The plumage, indeed, may be perfect, not a feather missing if you will, but a stiff attitude, an unstuffed throat, a distorted eye, a bad cut about the shoulders, in larger birds even an unstuffed cheek—these are blemishes which, obtruding themselves as they do on the fastidious eye of the connoisseur, have ere now consigned a "perfect specimen" to the dustbin, and, in my opinion, rightly too. One is almost inclined at times, after beholding some well-devilled effigy, to join the ranks of those who insist on keeping their birds as skins rather than subject them to the uncertain vicissitudes of the process so aptly designated "setting up."

Perhaps the most annoying fact connected with bird-stuffing is that the mistakes which spoil stuffed birds are such small ones, so easily avoided if one only gives time and care to the work. I have sat by and watched a good man ruin a bird simply because he would stroke the neck so lovingly while he had it turned inside out. My own belief is that any person possessed of moderately artistic tastes and perseverance can, if he will, become a good bird-stuffer; one of the best I ever knew had the clumsiest pair of hands imaginable. There is therefore no reason why collectors should be content with skins. Practically all that can be learnt from skins has been learnt already, and I think it the duty of those who now destroy bird-life to do their best to secure such reproductions as shall give most pleasure to any who may afterwards go to see them.

To begin with, the best way to secure rarities is to learn thoroughly the notes, shape, and flight of the common birds, and then shoot what you don't recognize. Always look carefully at a single shore-bird. One's efforts to preserve a bird should begin the moment it is shot. If only winged, capture it quickly, and, as Dr. Elliott Coues has well remarked, don't grab at its tail—you may get that and nothing else. When secured, don't let your admiration for its beauties induce you to paw it about. If it is bleeding, find the shot-holes at once and plug them with cotton-wool. If juices are running, let them drain for a bit, and then plug also the throat and nostrils, and if in no hurry lay the bird in the shade to stiffen.

Now for its receptacle. After many trials I have abandoned the time-honoured cone. In a cone the neck is sure to curl up, and, if juices do escape, the bird presents a sorry spectacle when removed. I now carry several pieces of stiff paper, and also a few pieces of cardboard about eight inches wide, each with two parallel bends in them at equal distances from the sides, such that with the aid of a tape they will easily form into a triangular pipe. I then put a piece of paper round the bird and pin it across the upper breast, tightly enough to prevent the shoulders slipping through. Next lay the bird enclosed in paper on the centre of the cardboard, the projecting ends of paper pointing upwards. Bend inwards the sides of the cardboard, arranging for the ends of the paper to pass through their apex, and tie a piece of tape round the whole. If carefully done, the bird's head will now lie perfectly free, the juices being unable to get at any feathers, and yet the whole will be protected from harm by the cardboard. This system sounds rather elaborate on paper, but it works very easily in the field—in fact, it is almost as quick as making a cone. If the bird is a large one, tie a handkerchief round its shoulders, the knot being on the breast, and carry it head downwards by the legs, taking care not to rub them. This is the safest of all ways to bring birds home, and though it spoils one's shooting for the time, it is worth doing also in the case of very rare small birds, a piece of paper and a pin being then substituted for the handkerchief. In ordinary weather two or three days is a good time to keep a bird before stuffing it. In the case of Warblers, &c.,

in the summer the difficulty is to stop them becoming decomposed too soon. All that can be done is to put some carbolic crystals in the throat, and, opening the skin of the vent, sprinkle plaster-of-Paris freely therein. I have heard of small Warblers being preserved *pro tem.* in a bottle of spirit.

Assuming that the bird has reached the stuffing table in safety, the less it is pawed about the better. Never upset the lay of the back feathers if you can help it, and above all don't stretch the skin of the neck and shoulders. A needle at the finish will do something towards putting bent feathers straight, but here, if anywhere, prevention is certainly better than cure. I always let the bird rest on a small piece of paper, so that I can turn the paper round instead of the bird. Be liberal with your plaster-of-Paris on the breast (the coarse sort with pinkish tinge is best), but don't start cleaning bloodstained feathers till you have finished skinning the head; juices may damage the very place you have just cleaned and necessitate a second washing.

To come to the all-important head—I say all-important, because on the amount of life you can infuse into it depends so largely the success of your efforts as a whole. If the head sticks (as Plover's and Woodpecker's generally do) when you try to turn it inside out, you may sometimes circumvent it by removing a triangular piece of skull, but in any case go to work steadily and keep your temper; a violent push or pull will leave you brandishing the head in one hand and the remainder of the skin in the other—a state of things which looks foolish, though it is not necessarily fatal. If gentle suasion fails to entice the head through the aperture, you must slit the skin along the skull and get it out there, and this is generally needful in the case of Ducks. While the head is turned inside out, the difficulty of keeping the breast-feathers unstained by the neck can be got over by resting the latter on a piece of paper with a slit in it. The neck goes into the slit, and the head lies on the paper beyond. All the lower part of the skull must be cut away, and the brains extracted from the bottom. The cheek bones can be partly cut away also, and their loss subsequently compensated for by the insertion of wadding through the eyeholes and mouth, or they may be left in and clay modelled round them to fill up all cavities. In any case, remember that though the head may look perfect when just stuffed, the cheeks and also the space between the eye and beak always tend to shrink in the drying, and they must be very carefully filled up with cotton-wool or clay. If the cheek bones are removed, it will be difficult to keep the tow in the skull; it must be bound round with cotton. As soon as the head is turned back, at once restore the natural lie of the feathers with a needle, and, if you like, insert the eyes. Insert them with the utmost care: there is much in a life-like eye.

The throat must, of course, be stuffed as well as the cheeks, and it is best done after the wire has been passed through the skull. Most people spend much time in cleaning and wrapping up the thigh-bones and long inner bones of the wing; it is unnecessary in the smaller birds. The majority seldom show much of their thighs, and the part they do show is so thin that the wire running beside the bone is quite sufficient stuffing in itself. Therefore cut away half the thigh-bone *after* you have got the wire through. Again, instead of cleaning and wrapping the wing-bones, cut them away, and bind a lump of tow on the back of the body to compensate for their loss; the effect is better, and you save time. A straight back looks well in a barrack-yard, a round one in a stuffed bird. Moreover, this rotundity helps the set of the wings. Before leaving the subject of skinning, I would impress upon the beginner not to abandon a bird as spoilt if he has the misfortune to relieve it of its head or tail. The tail can be put in afterwards with a wire, and if slightly cocked will look quite natural. It is the same with the head; you need only push it down the neck-wire into the shoulders and put your bird in an attitude of repose.

Stuffing is a more difficult task than skinning, and it is here that the artistic element comes in. On the whole, corrosive sublimate mixed with methylated spirit until it just does not leave a deposit on a black feather, is the best preservative; but it is very poisonous, and the skin begins to lose its flexibility directly it is anointed with it, so much so that I generally wash it over afterwards with water to get it properly relaxed again. Equal parts of burnt alum, naphthaline and tannin form an innocuous preparation much recommended by some. They use it dry, and rub it into the skin.

Provided that you have your lump on the back, it is better to get the body too small rather than too big; you can stuff chopped tow into the flanks as you sew up. If the skin won't meet across the breast, you may slit the sides beneath the wings, and then it will. I consider it best to have a wooden back to one's cases, because it enables you to aim at making the "show" side perfect rather than both moderate. This advice may savour of the well-known motto that "What isn't seen need not be clean," but, as a fact, the slight turn of the head, which infuses such life into the near side, must always be done at the expense of expression on the other; and it seems best to recognize this truism at once and act upon it.

Be careful about the angle of the legs; next to the head they do most towards the making or marring of the bird. If walking, let the front leg be well forward. Most birds of prey, Harriers excepted, show the foot only when resting. In the matter of attitudes, throw over the stereotyped and indulge in striking positions from the start. One is always told to go straight to Nature, and so you may if there is any chance of your meeting it, which in the case of most rare birds there isn't. I therefore always carry about with me a rough sketch-book containing copies of pictures culled from the choicest bird-books, and very valuable I have found them. A bird running or settling with uplifted wings adds a life-like element to a shore-birds' case. A victim beneath its foot, with the blood represented by sealing-wax, is an obvious addition to any raptorial bird. A badly damaged breast should be hidden by making the bird lie down if it happens to be a shore-bird, and the operation of wing-cleaning is sometimes a useful antidote to a battered head.

Above all things, don't hurry this part of the operations; it is more important than the skinning, but one is apt to get slack after the latter, and the bird is rushed into the first position that seems to suit. If time presses, it is better to fill the skin with damp cotton-wool, and put it aside until one has leisure to attend to the stuffing with proper care. When the bird is stuffed, keep your eye on it for some days. The skin will shrink as it dries, and it is necessary to continually hitch up the parts about the neck and shoulders with a needle, so long as this process is going on. Sometimes, in hot weather, the skin around the beak may have received too little of the preservative, and show a tendency to decay. If so, anoint it with corrosive or benzine, otherwise the feathers will come out *en masse*. If the birds have to travel, bore holes in their stands, four in each, and corresponding ones in the bottom of a cardboard box. Pass two strings through each stand, and then through the box, and tie firmly on the outside.

A word on alterations and repairs. More can be done to resurrect inferior specimens than is generally supposed. I once bought a Harrier, which at the time could have been used only as a scarecrow; it is now a respectable bird. In such cases half measures are useless. Don't trust to a relaxing box. . More satisfactory results are to be got out of a basin of water with vinegar in it. To do any good, you must get the skin *thoroughly* under control, and this is the most effective way of doing it. When the skin has been soaked long enough, it can be kneaded inside with a piece of smooth wood, and afterwards rubbed with an old shaving-brush dipped in water. The feathers will then become fairly obedient to the modeller. The danger, as usual, centres round the throat and cheeks; the feathers there may rot out, and care must be taken that this part is sub-merged for much less time than the body. The above-mentioned Harrier enjoyed a forty-eight hours' bath, and was subsequently dried with plaster-of-Paris. It was a success so far as the body was concerned, but I lost feathers from the throat. This loss, however, is not of necessity irreparable. I detached others from the unseen side, and, gumming them one above the other on tissue paper so as to overlap, inserted a passable imitation of the original side. Such desperate remedies are needful only in the case of a rare bird which cannot be matched. In ordinary circumstances, the injured back, tail, or whatever it may be, can be got from the bird of the same species and inserted whole. If it is the case of a few feathers only being missing, or of an unseemly depression down the centre of the breast, the evil can be remedied by the insertion of single feathers. Cut off their bases, lift up the feathers just above the gap, and with a forceps thrust in the cut feather with a little paste at the end. You can thus easily get it to stick where it is wanted, and the gap disappears forthwith.

An operation which I once performed with some success on an Avocet was the removal of a damaged inch of neck. This was accomplished by simple cutting, with little real difficulty, and the head was then forced down the neck-wire, so that the Avocet now stands in an attitude of repose, with its head drawn into its shoulders. Beaks and claws can be repaired with wax, and then painted. Throats and cheeks can be stuffed without relaxing the whole skin, if a piece of wet cotton-wool be tied round the head for a couple of days. It is, however, a ticklish operation at all times. The eye must be extracted, and the skin beneath and on either side carefully worked with a smooth flat strip of wood, cotton-wool being inserted in the cavities thus formed. The greatest difficulty lies in detaching the skin between the eye and beak from the bone to which it will adhere, and only in the case of largish birds can one hope to meet with any great measure of success. If you do venture at all, again I say, be bold but don't hurry.

CHAPTER XXVII.

BIRD PROTECTION.

A CHAPTER on the subject of bird protection is not unlikely to be received with scepticism when coming from the pen of that *bête noire* of all fashionable naturalists, the Collector. But without laying any claim to an impregnable position, so far as bias is concerned, I propose, nevertheless, to make one or two remarks and suggestions on a subject now so frequently discussed. The persistent slaughter of birds towards the end of the last century, and the consequent decrease in the number of our British species, created in due time a perfectly natural and justifiable reaction; but, as is the way with all reactions, there seems at the present moment a danger of common sense being swamped in a blind zeal for protection, which is likely in the end to overshoot itself. Witness the recent successful protest of the Aldeburgh fishermen.

Let us see how matters actually stand. The birds of prey and the Raven at the present moment are a class reduced to the verge of extinction, but unless game-preservers can be induced, either by persuasion or by legal penalties, to spare them, their case must be regarded as past curing—they are doomed. It is a thousand pities, but it is so, and if the ravages of the game-preserver are to go on unchecked, the killing of an odd bird or so by collectors is a matter of very small moment, after all.

Of the remaining British birds, despite the talk on the subject, very few are in real danger. Drainage and land-reclaiming have banished for ever as breeding species such birds as the Ruff, the Avocet, the Black-tailed Godwit, the Black Tern, the Bittern, and the Bustard. The shooting of such stragglers as turn up on migration in the autumn does not make the slightest difference to the chance of their breeding in England again. They belong to another branch of the family, with another habitat and another breeding area.

We come next to a small class of birds which still breed sparingly in the British Isles, and whose numbers, in two cases at all events, are unlikely ever to be recruited from abroad. These two are the Bearded

B. C. Arnold. Pinxt.]

[West Newman.

A RARE VISITOR FROM AMERICA. *(Buff-breasted Sandpiper.)*

Tit and the Dartford Warbler; and the others that belong to somewhat the same class are the Great Crested Grebe, the Dotterel, the Roseate Tern, and the Chough. These birds need protection badly, and it is not too late to give it them. If the existing laws concerning the close season were rigorously enforced, three of them would be protected enough, as they leave this country in the autumn. Special measures should be taken in the case of the first two and the last.

Our other birds may be divided into two classes. First come the rarer migrants. Concerning the shooting of these stragglers there is always the greatest outcry, whereas they are just the ones that matter least. There is no chance of their becoming British species in the proper sense of the term; they are mostly common enough in their real habitat, and the shooting of these odd birds makes no difference whatever to the chance of their appearing in England another year. They have got separated from their species and proper home, and are doomed. I say, without hesitation, that the best fate that can befall them is to be shot by someone who can appreciate their beauties. Bluethroats must often have visited the Norfolk coast before Dr. Power discovered them. How many people got any pleasure out of those visits? If I meet a Dartford Warbler it is to me a sacred bird, but if I meet a Bluethroat I shoot it, to present it to one of the numerous institutions which are only too glad to get a specimen of the bird. It is thus seen by more people than if it passed another week in England on its way to a lingering death.

Secondly, there come the bulk of our commoner birds; I doubt whether any of these have become rarer in recent years. The establishment of the existing close season seems to have just met the case so far as they are concerned. Birds like Hawfinches and Goldfinches are unquestionably on the increase in nearly every part of England.

Such is the situation as it stands to-day. What are the chief dangers that threaten the birds, and what are the existing measures and proposals designed to grapple with them?

Passing by as much exaggerated the danger which awaits our threatened species from the amateur collector, on the ground that he is usually satisfied with a single pair, I would suggest that the birds have most to fear from three classes of individual—the shore-shooter, who goes out for mere slaughter; the man who shoots to provide the trade, whether it be that of the London naturalist or the milliner; and the ordinary country bird-catcher.

To counteract the efforts of these worthies, there is at present a law protecting nearly all birds from the beginning of February until the end of July, and County Councils have powers to extend this close season in their counties, and to protect special birds throughout the year.

Before discussing the working of these measures, I would lay it down as an axiom that all such laws, to be effective, must be supported by a certain amount of public sympathy, and that, too, the sympathy of the men on the spot, and, above all, of the better type of amateur collector; he perhaps can do more than anyone else to aid or nullify them. As matters now stand, both collectors and professional fowlers are for all practical purposes agreed in upholding the law. They recognize that it is for the common good that the birds, while breeding, should be protected. But there has been, especially on the coast, much ill feeling aroused by the extension of the close season in some counties to August. The collector feels that his chance, small as it was, of securing a summer-plumaged Wader has been much reduced; the fowler, noticing that Duck and Snipe, which frequent the fresh marshes of the neighbouring landowner, may now be shot, while his Curlew or Whimbrel must be left severely alone, can hardly be blamed for suggesting that this is a case of one law for the rich and another for the poor; while the villager who was accustomed to provide lodgings for collectors finds himself suddenly docked of what he had come to regard as a regular part of his income, and the local tradesman also sees his profits seriously curtailed. In fact, the village is hit all round, and but for the fact that bicycling has lately opened up these districts and thereby increased the number of casual August holiday-seekers, the outcry would have been far greater than it is.

Letters have recently appeared in the papers, from well-meaning but, I think, misguided bird-lovers, suggesting that September also should be included in the close time. For this proposal there is practically nothing to be said. By the time August is out quite sufficient birds have passed south to provide a breeding stock for next year, and the remainder may well be left to take their chance. Again, if the collector is to be driven away from the villages in September, very real hardship will be 'inflicted on their inhabitants. He is the only person who goes there so late; the ordinary tripper has found his way back to town; and, lastly, the seashore is the poor man's natural hunting-ground. Why, while his rich neighbours are shooting their Partridges, should he be deprived of a sport not one whit inferior to theirs? While, if it comes to mere sentimentality, I suppose a Partridge feels a shot as much as a Wader does. As for the rarities, even now it is easy enough, if one wants to do it, to bribe local shooters to get them in the close season; and if September is included, no doubt bribery will become more common than it is, and thus many naturally law-abiding villagers will be constantly tempted to transgress.

Far better have the collector shooting openly in September than his gold working secretly against the law.

What is really wanted is not any more *general* measures, but some effective method of dealing with the man who massacres Terns (they are in fact the only sea-birds foolish enough to allow themselves to be massacred) from mere love of slaughter, and the man who kills them for the trade. I would suggest that it should be made a penal offence to shoot more than one pair of Terns of the same species on the same day, and that it should be a penal offence also to offer for sale the skins of any bird on the British list (whether imported from abroad or not) in a milliner's shop. If these two laws were made, we should hear little on the subject of slaughtered sea-birds.

The important thing, to my mind, is that there should be scattered about, here and there in our island, a few well-chosen bird sanctuaries, where a gun is never fired, and where the birds can breed in peace. The Farne Islands and Wicken Fen are cases in point. The New Forest might well be made another, and if one or two Broads known as resorts of the Bearded Tit, and perhaps some recognized haunt of the Dartford Warbler, were added, there would be no need to meddle with any seaside places, which, after all, are seldom more than temporary stopping-places for the birds.

Finally, I think that County Councils should specially protect throughout the year certain birds in real danger of extermination, and *pace* the game-preserver, the first of these should be the birds of prey. They should be authorized at the same time to grant licences to enable persons, who could prove that they were collecting for a public museum, to secure a single pair of any species that it required.

It has been suggested that bird-photography should supersede all bird-collecting, and the idea is attractive at first sight. I doubt, however, whether this pursuit will ever satisfy many persons for any length of time. In the first place, the results are hardly worth the trouble involved in acquiring them. They are interesting in a way, no doubt, but put them side by side with a drawing by Thorburn or Lodge, and they sink into insignificance at once. Again, the great naturalist has been evolved in most cases out of the boy-collector, and this is, in my opinion, the natural order of things. A boy generally has some elements of sport in him, but very seldom real artistic leanings. If you turn him on to the camera at the start, he grows tired of it in a few months and his interest in natural history evaporates. But set him to stuff birds and collect birds' eggs, and he will not, at all events, grow up a prig, and he may develop into a second Waterton unawares. The harm he will do is infinitesimal. In fifteen years I have only known one rare bird and one rare nest obtained by the unaided efforts of boys.

As he gets older he makes more notes and kills fewer birds; he has got an interesting hobby, and he may write an interesting book, but he will not necessarily be a monster who collects "for love of killing," or "to make money out of it"! He may even find himself the possessor of a little common sense, a quality in which his detractors have shown themselves on occasions strangely deficient.

As a specimen of the rubbish that can be written by an enthusiastic bird protector, and of the astounding simplicity which he can exhibit, I give below a cutting which appeared not long since in a widely circulated London newspaper, one which reflects as little credit on the intelligence of the editor as on that of the author himself, since the absurdity of it is apparent at a glance. Speaking of a sale of rare eggs, including those of the St. Kilda Wren, at Stevens' auction rooms, and protesting against the taking of these eggs, the writer solemnly affirms: "There were five nests containing twenty-three eggs of the St. Kilda Wren, and they sold in all for £2 16s. The natives of St. Kilda protest strongly against dealers taking these eggs. They depend upon the birds very largely for their food supply, and barter feathers and oil for footstuffs and manufactured goods. It is feared that the breeding stock of the native Wren will soon be exhausted." If words mean anything at all, we are apparently to regard the natives of St. Kilda as persons who, by some occult process, extract oil from the local Wren and afterwards exchange it for "footstuffs." It would be interesting to hear how many native Wrens it takes to produce a gallon of oil. Again, these hardy fowlers, a race generally credited with the power of masticating and digesting salted Puffins and Fulmars, must be pictured henceforth as a society of epicures, who regale themselves on the daintiest of entrées— St. Kilda Wrens *in aspic*—much, I suppose, as the Romans used to delight in figpeckers, or the modern Frenchman in his frogs and snails!

WEST, NEWMAN AND CO., PRINTERS, HATTON GARDEN, LONDON.

Lightning Source UK Ltd.
Milton Keynes UK
UKOW041052241012

201110UK00001B/80/P